MACMILLAN MODERN DRAMATISTS

Macmillan Modern Dramatists
Series Editors: Bruce and Adele King

Published titles

Reed Anderson, *Federico García Lorca*
Clive Barker, *British Alternative Theatre*
Normand Berlin, *Eugene O'Neill*
Michael Billington, *Alan Ayckbourn (2nd ed.)*
Roger Boxill, *Tennessee Williams*
David Bradby and David Williams, *Directors' Theatre*
John Bull, *New British Political Dramatists*
Dennis Carroll, *David Mamet*
Neil Carson, *Arthur Miller*
Maurice Charney, *Joe Orton*
Ruby Cohn, *New American Dramatists, 1960-1990*
Bernard F. Dukore, *American Dramatists, 1918-1945*
Bernard F. Dukore, *Harold Pinter (2nd ed.)*
Michael Etherton, *Contemporary Irish Dramatists*
Arthur Ganz, *George Bernard Shaw*
G.K. Gianakaris, *Peter Shaffer*
James Gibbs, *Wole Soyinka*
Frances Gray, *John Arden*
Penny Griffin, *Pinero and Jones*
David Hirst, *Edward Bond*
David Hirst, *Dario Fo and Franca Rame*
Helene Keyssar, *Feminist Theatre*
Bettina L. Knapp, *French Theatre 1918-1939*
Thomas Leabhart, *Modern and Post-modern Mime*
Charles Lyons, *Samuel Beckett*
Gerry McCarthy, *Edward Albee*
Margery Morgan, *August Strindberg*
Karol Rosen, *Sam Shepard*
Jeanette L. Savona, *Jean Genet*
Laurence Senelick, *Anton Chekhov*
Theodore Shank, *American Alternative Theatre*
James Simmons, *Sean O'Casey*
Peter Skrine, *Hauptmann, Wedekind and Schnitzler*
Ronald Speirs, *Bertolt Brecht*
David Thomas, *Henrik Ibsen*
Dennis Walder, *Athol Fugard*
Thomas Whitaker, *Tom Stoppard*
Katharine Worth, *Oscar Wilde*

Further titles in preparation

MACMILLAN MODERN DRAMATISTS

TENNESSEE WILLIAMS

Roger Boxill
Professor of English
City College
City University of New York

MACMILLAN

First published 1987 by
THE MACMILLAN PRESS LTD
Houndmills, Basingstoke, Hampshire RG21 2XS
and London
Companies and representatives
throughout the world

ISBN 0–333–30884–0
ISBN 0–333–30885–9

A catalogue record for this book is available
from the British Library.

Printed in Hong Kong

Reprinted 1988, 1992

For
KATHLEEN BOXILL and LEILA F. BOXILL

Contents

A Note on the Texts

A Williams play in print often differs substantially from the script used in its original production. Revivals have sometimes made further changes, and in several cases two or more versions have been published. Unless otherwise noted, the version contained in *The Theatre of Tennessee Williams*, published in New York by New Directions in seven volumes, 1971–81 (hereafter abbreviated as Williams, *Theatre*) provides the basis for discussion here. The date in my text following the title of a play is that of the professional premiere (pre-Broadway try-outs apart) or the first edition, whichever is earlier.

List of Plates

Phillips as Alma and Tod Andrews as John. Courtesy: Culver Pictures, New York.

7. *Summer and Smoke*, New York, 1948. Alma bids farewell to Eternity. Margaret Phillips as Alma. Courtesy: Culver Pictures, New York.

8. *Cat on a Hot Tin Roof*, New York, 1955. Barbara Bel Geddes as Margaret and Ben Gazzara as Brick. Courtesy: Culver Pictures, New York.

9. *Cat on a Hot Tin Roof*, MGM film, 1958. Burl Ives as Big Daddy and Paul Newman as Brick. Courtesy: MGM/UA Entertainment Company.

10. *A Streetcar Named Desire*, Warner Bros film, 1951. Vivien Leigh as Blanche. Courtesy: Culver Pictures, New York.

Acknowledgements

I would like first to thank my friends Margaret and Arthur Ganz without whose early encouragement I would probably not have undertaken this study nor without their enduring kindness and good counsel brought it to completion. I will always be grateful to my teacher, Eric Bentley, from whom I learned how to think about dramatic art and how best to define Williams's contribution to its history. I am grateful to Anthony Friedmann, Beth Glick, Arthur Golden, Michael Goldman, Leo Hamalian, Judith Hennessee, Stanford Myers, David Rubin, and Peter Strachan for their generous advice and staunch support. I would also like to express my appreciation to Andreas Brown for his help with the bibliography, to Mitch Douglas for giving me access to unpublished and unproduced material, to Lyle Leverich for his biographical corrections, to David Beams for his careful index, to Kay Krane and Leila F. Boxill for checking the proofs, and to the City University of New York for a timely fellowship award.

The author and publishers acknowledge New Directions

Acknowledgements

'Heavenly Grass' from IN THE WINTER OF CITIES. Copyright 1946 by Tennessee Williams.

CAMINO REAL. Copyright 1948, 1953 by Tennessee Williams.

THE TWO-CHARACTER PLAY. Copyright © 1969, 1973, 1976 by Tennessee Williams.

BATTLE OF ANGELS. Copyright 1940 by Tennessee Williams.

Editors' Preface

The *Macmillan Modern Dramatists* is an international series of introductions to major and significant nineteenth- and twentieth-century dramatists, movements and new forms of drama in Europe, Great Britain, America and new nations such as Nigeria and Trinidad. Besides new studies of great and influential dramatists of the past, the series includes volumes on contemporary authors, recent trends in the theatre and on many dramatists, such as writers of farce, who have created theatre 'classics' while being neglected by literary criticism. The volumes in the series devoted to individual dramatists include a biography, a survey of the plays, and detailed analysis of the most significant plays, along with discussion, where relevant, of the political, social, historical and theatrical context. The authors of the volumes, who are involved with theatre as playwrights, directors, actors, teachers and critics, are concerned with the plays as theatre and discuss such matters as performance, character interpretation and staging, along with themes and contexts.

BRUCE KING

ADELE KING

1
Introduction and Life

Time is short and it doesn't return again. It is slipping away while I write this and while you read it, and the monosyllable of the clock is Loss, loss, loss, unless you devote your heart to its opposition.

('On a Streetcar Named Success')

The myth of the Old South is a pastoral romance, the myth of its fall a pastoral elegy. Both the romance and the elegy are manifestations of the American agrarian myth: the underlying notion in the national literature of an earthly paradise in the unspoiled landscape of the New World. In turn, the agrarian myth is only one among many statements of the universal human longing for an ideal order of being denied by the harsh realities of life and time, among which are the legends of Camelot, Eden and the Golden Age.

Tennessee Williams is an elegiac writer, a poet of nostalgia who laments the loss of a past idealised in the memory. As the leading dramatist of the Southern

1

Renaissance in American letters, he draws on the myth of the Old South. As a homosexual, he makes his version of it a feminine dream. His most memorable characters are women, faded belles such as Amanda Wingfield, Alma Winemiller, and Blanche DuBois, whose old-fashioned manners and charm suggest a wishful recollection of privileged antebellum life. In the fond vision of cotillions, elegant conversations and gentlemen callers there is little to indicate male pursuits. Even the name of the DuBois estate, Belle Reve, is ungrammatically feminine. The men, or at any rate the leading men of the major plays – Stanley Kowalski, Jim O'Connor, and John Buchanan – live for today. The recurrent conflict in Williams, between animal promiscuity and ladylike fastidiousness, between the physical and the spiritual needs, overlays the conflict between the painful present and the ideal past. Sexual opposition is finally only one side of the more fundamental one between reality and *rêve*.

Time, waster of youth and beauty, despoiler of dreams, is the enemy of us all. The familiar subject of Shakespeare's sonnets and Keats's odes, however, receives a greater sexual emphasis in Williams, arising from unresolved conflict in the writer's personality. The decline of the Williams family from prominence among the early settlers of Tennessee mirrors the fate of the South. The playwright's own upbringing seemed to him a still greater fall. He was unable to make the transition from sheltered childhood to self-confident adulthood during the adolescent period of sexual discovery. The remainder of his life only reinforced his impression of the brief bloom and long decay of things. Consequently, his plays are both elegiac and confessional. Like his most important predecessor in the American theatre, Eugene O'Neill, Williams told his own story – or anyhow some version of it –

again and again, in a lifelong effort to come to terms with his family.

He told it not only in the muted tones of *The Glass Menagerie* and *Vieux Carré* but also in the Gothic chiaroscuro of *Orpheus Descending* and *Sweet Bird of Youth*. The tarnished Adonises with 'the charm of the defeated' who are castrated and lynched at Easter or cannibalised abroad in summer are masks of the self in the condition of simultaneous punishment and revolt. The degradation of the beautiful or, conversely, the apotheosis of the sordid produces a nightmarish quality in Williams's violent plays that allies him with Jean Genet.

Williams's comic side is escapist or self-belittling. The wildly triumphant endings of *You Touched Me!* and *The Rose Tattoo* are only a step away from the plainly fantastic ones of *Stairs to the Roof* and *The Knightly Quest*; in the last two the solution to the problems of the world is to leave the planet. That there is no remedy on earth for the pain of existence also produces the black humour of the 'slapstick tragedies', *The Gnädiges Fräulein* and *The Mutilated*. In Williams's most familiar work comedy punctures protective illusions and undermines human dignity. Tom Wingfield ridicules his mother's girlish airs and maternal earnestness; Big Daddy makes a mockery of his birthday celebration; the wisecracking Kowalski overturns Blanche's pretensions in a classic comic duel of body and soul. The sadness of life inherent in the course of eroding time is not reduced but reaffirmed, grounded in reality by the writer's wise chuckle, knowing smile, or raucous laugh.

Williams, who found his voice for the theatre in the 1940s, belongs to the first generation of dramatists brought up on the movies instead of on plays, as the strong influence of film on his stagecraft shows. The journalistic realism of the drama of social protest that preceded him gave way to a more frankly evocative, symbolic or 'poetic' theatre marked by Williams's command of Southern speech. Having begun as a writer of poetry and short fiction, he derived his dramatic structure from the lyric form of the modern short story rather than from the narrative form of the modern drama as established by Ibsen.

At the height of his fame Williams wrote that a new tradition was taking root in the theatre, which he called 'the play of sensibility'. It could be recognised by 'the fine texture, the sensitive surface that are found more often in stories and novels, the poetic detail and the quiet progression of serious fiction'. His comments appear in the programme for the production of Donald Windham's *The Starless Air*, which he directed at the Dallas Playhouse in 1953. In praising Windham's kind of play, Williams was defining his own, or at any rate the kind of play for which he is best remembered.

Williams learned theatrical symbolism from Lorca, sentimentality from Saroyan, and sexual warfare from Strindberg and D. H. Lawrence. His anti-naturalist experiments, most notably the dream play *Camino Real* and the ghost play *Clothes for a Summer Hotel*, also derive from Strindberg. His violence and brooding lie in the Gothic tradition which runs from Melville, Hawthorne and Poe down to Faulkner, McCullers and Capote. But his surface naturalism, his blend of sadness and mockery, and his apparently casual handling of plot come from the drama as well as from the short fiction of his acknowledged master, Chekhov, who fifty years before him had already written elegiac plays about the passing of a rural aristocracy.

Williams's attitude toward the old order is, like Chekhov's, ambivalent. *The Cherry Orchard* shows charm and breeding allied with childishness and indolence.

Streetcar shows sensitivity and cultivation allied with dependency and decadence. The playwright who, ten years before the Civil Rights Amendment, refused to allow his plays to be performed in segregated theatres was not a reactionary. The myth of the Old South was only a dream; but it was a dream he could not quite let go. This explains the poignancy of Amanda Wingfield, a middle-class woman who thinks she was Scarlett O'Hara in her youth. It adds irony to the plight of the homeless Blanche DuBois, whose ancestral home was lost, not because the Confederacy was defeated in the Civil War, but because the men of her family squandered their fortune on debauchery. The past was far from ideal when it was the present, a point that Williams often makes by showing the pathetic delusions of his nostalgic characters. Brick Pollitt cannot abide the thought that his friendship with the deceased Skipper was less than pure; Violet Venable thinks her son's life was a poem; Lady Torrance remembers her father's outdoor speakeasy as a garden of love.

The theme of illusion and reality merges with the theme of past and present to produce the elegiac play of sensibility, created by Chekhov at the end of the nineteenth century, adopted by Williams in the middle of the twentieth, and handed on to his followers William Inge, Carson McCullers, Horton Foote and Lanford Wilson. Its vogue, however, lasted little more than a decade. The Actors Studio in New York, which learned its method of playing Williams and his school from Stanislavsky's method of playing Chekhov, lost influence in the 1960s as the play of sensibility gave way to the theatre of the absurd. The period of the studio's dominance in the history of the American stage coincides with the era of Tennessee Williams.

*　　　*　　　*

Tennessee Williams died on 25 February 1983 in his suite at the Elysée, a small hotel in east midtown Manhattan. He would have been seventy-two the following month. A plastic bottle cap of the type used to cover eyedrops or nasal spray had somehow lodged in his throat and choked him to death. He was a pudgy little man with a roguish grin, a soft handshake, and a gravelly drawl. The searching, needy look in his eyes betrayed an inordinate vulnerability that he tried hard to cover up with an explosive laugh that always continued for a bit too long. He was an obsessive worker, a hypochondriac, a habitual swimmer, an amateur painter, a frequent traveller and a multi-millionaire. He left all his assets in a trust fund for his only sister, who has been institutionalised since her youth. After her death the bulk of his estate is to be given to the University of the South for the support of its programme in creative writing.

He was born Thomas Lanier Williams III on 26 March 1911 in Columbus, Mississippi, an old town on the Tombigbee River deep in the American South. He was the second of the three children of Cornelius Coffin ('C. C.') Williams, a travelling shoe salesman, and Edwina Dakin ('Miss Edwina') Williams, a minister's daughter. Their first child, a daughter, Rose, had been born two years earlier. Their third, a son, Dakin, would be born eight years later.

C. C. was a forceful, blustering man of illustrious lineage gone to seed. He enjoyed the life of a Mississippi drummer – the travelling, the all-night poker games, the 'light ladies'. He had been to a military prep school, briefly studied law, and served in the Spanish–American War as a second lieutenant. Among his forebears were John Williams, US senator from Tennessee to the Fourteenth Congress; John Sevier, first governor of the state; and the poet Sidney Lanier. The first Thomas Lanier Williams was prominent in the government of Tennessee before it became a state.

The second Thomas Lanier Williams, however, paternal grandfather of the playwright, squandered the family fortune in unsuccessful campaigns for governor, and the old Williams residence in Knoxville was turned into an orphanage.

Miss Edwina was a beautiful, sexually fastidious Southern belle who lived on the verge of hysteria. There were a number of mental breakdowns in the history of her family, and she herself became a patient in a psychiatric ward later in life. Her immediate background was benign and genteel. Her father, the Reverend Walter E. Dakin, was an Episcopal clergyman with a taste for bridge and travel. Her mother, Rose Otte Dakin ('Grand'), was a woman of great generosity of heart, who taught the piano and violin. In 'Facts about Me' (1958) Williams remarks that he derived from his mother and father an uneasy combination of the Puritan and the Cavalier which helps to account for the thematic conflicts in much of his work.[1]

Because C. C. spent most of his time on the road, Miss Edwina and the children lived in a series of Episcopal rectories, the parish residences of the Reverend Walter Dakin in Columbus, Memphis, Canton, and Clarksdale. Williams remembered those early peaceful years as a summer's idyll. The climate was warm, and there were grounds outdoors for play. His protective mother and grandmother were near; his sensitive and highly spirited sister, Rose, with whom he felt the closest of ties, was his constant companion by day; and in the evening the children would sit at the feet of their beloved black nurse, Ozzie, and listen to tales of wonder and mystery. His father seemed to intrude upon the tranquillity of the household when he returned from the road every two weeks, a massive, fearful presence in contrast with the slight figure of the kindly grandfather, whom the boy would sometimes accompany on parish calls.

At the age of five Williams suffered an almost fatal attack of what was probably diphtheria and Bright's Disease. He lost the use of his legs for nearly two years. Kept out of school, in fact bed-ridden most of the time, he was attended by Ozzie, Grand and Miss Edwina. The illness subjected him to a prolongation of infantile dependence that proved formative. When he regained his health, his boyish rambunctiousness was gone, replaced by a new shyness and effeminacy; but out of the need to survive he had learned the trick of escape from life's adversity into his rich imaginings.

When the First World War ended in 1918, C. C. was promoted to sales manager of the St Louis branch of the International Shoe Company. What seemed to be an advancement in the fortunes of the Williams family was instead a change for the worse. Miss Edwina, who had grown up in a house with servants, had to teach herself to cook in St Louis. C. C. did not like his desk job, missed the road and took to drink. Eventually he required treatment for alcoholism. To the children, life in the busy metropolis after the sleepy rural towns from which they had come seemed like an expulsion from Eden. They were teased and snubbed for their Southern speech and manners. Tom was persecuted as a sissy into the bargain. Even at home his father called him 'Miss Nancy' because he preferred books and movies to outdoor games.

The movies were an escape from the pains of rejection. But the silent images that flickered in the darkness had beckoned the sensitive child from the beginning. On one occasion his mother had to hold him down when he wanted to get up and join the characters on the screen. In St Louis he became an avid movie fan. He won a contest in his teens for a review of *Stella Dallas* sponsored by Loew's State Theatre. He read movie magazines, and in later years, when he could afford to, would buy them by the half dozen.

Williams withdrew even further into himself at the time of his sister's puberty. As he reveals in his autobiographical short story 'The Resemblance between a Violin Case and a Coffin' (1950)[2] the beginning of adulthood for her meant the end for him of his only close childhood companionship. He and Rose had become more intimate since the move to St Louis, allies in a hostile city. The sudden and mysterious change in her seemed a rejection that left him with a deepened sense of being alone; furthermore, his brother, eight years his junior, was plainly favoured by C. C. Under the circumstances, it was an inspiration for Miss Edwina to give her first son the present of a typewriter. As the author explains in his Foreword to *Sweet Bird of Youth* (1959), it was out of the same need to escape into an imaginary world during his childhood illness that he began to write during his early adolescence:

At the age of fourteen I discovered writing as an escape from a world of reality in which I felt acutely uncomfortable. It immediately became my place of retreat, my cave, my refuge. From what? From being called a sissy by neighborhood kids, and Miss Nancy by my father, because I would rather read books in my grandfather's large and classical library than play marbles and baseball and other normal kid games, a result of a severe childhood illness and of excessive attachment to the female members of my family, who had coaxed me back into life.

Williams, who had still never seen a professional production of a play, produced poems, essays, and short stories. At the age of sixteen he won five dollars for third prize in a contest sponsored by *Smart Set* magazine on the topic 'Can a Good Wife Be a Good Sport?' (1927). It was his first professional publication. While Williams served his literary apprenticeship in St Louis, Eugene O'Neill dominated the stage in New York, and simultaneously a group of poets and critics at Vanderbilt University – notably, John Crowe Ransom, Donald Davidson, Robert Penn Warren and Allen Tate – engendered the Southern Literary Renaissance in Nashville. Their magazine *The Fugitive* (1922–5) marks the beginning of a movement that was to break bounds in poetry, fiction, drama and criticism. The Fugitives looked back with longing to an agrarian South. Their nostalgic attitude underlies Williams's plays; their name is a key word in his dramatic vocabulary. *The Fugitive Kind* (1937) is the title of an early unpublished play about derelicts in a St Louis flophouse. It is also the title of the screen version of *Orpheus Descending* (1960). In both cases it refers to characters who are out of place in the modern world of commerce and industry.

Important novels by the two leading writers of the Southern Renaissance, William Faulkner's *The Sound and the Fury* and Thomas Wolfe's *Look Homeward, Angel*, appeared in 1929, the year that Williams entered the University of Missouri at Columbia with the intention of majoring in journalism. He won small prizes for poetry and prose and gained honourable mention in drama contests for the one-act plays *Beauty is the Word* and *Hot Milk at Three in the Morning*; but he was only a fair student and he failed ROTC (Reserve Officers Training Corps) in his third year. His irate father, who took great pride in the military tradition of the family, removed him from college and put him to work in the warehouse of the International Shoe Company back in St Louis. It was early in the Depression.

For the next three years Williams worked in the warehouse as a shipping-clerk. At night and on weekends he continued to write poems and short stories, fortifying himself with cigarettes and black coffee. Eventually his health gave way. In 1935 he had a nervous breakdown, possibly a minor stroke as well, and the paralysis of his legs partly returned. The immediate cause of the nervous attack was heartbreak. He learned that the woman he loved had just married someone else. Hazel Kramer and Williams had been high-school sweethearts who had planned to go away to college together before C. C., disapproving of the match, prevented them. Williams said in his *Memoirs* that the relationship with Hazel Kramer was the deepest extrafamilial attachment of his life. In the beginning of his freshman year at Missouri, he wrote to propose to her, but by that time her feelings had changed.

After a brief stay in the hospital, Williams went to visit his grandparents in Memphis where the Reverend Walter Dakin was now retired. Over the summer of his convalescence he met a neighbour, Bernice Dorothy Shapiro, who was working with a little theatre group called the Garden Players. She invited him to try his hand at a play. The result was the Shapiro–Williams collaboration *Cairo, Shanghai, Bombay!* (1935) – a one-act comedy about sailors on shore leave. The modest success of the little comedy was therapeutic.

Williams found that he liked writing plays and that he liked the immediate, visible reaction of an audience to his work. When he returned home in the autumn he began working for another little theatre group, the Mummers of St Louis, who, as he recalls in 'Something Wild' (1947), were charged with 'that kind of excessive romanticism which is youth and which is the best and purest part of life'. The Mummers were a Bohemian crowd of eager amateurs less interested in doing the classics than in trying the new. What was new at the time was the drama of social protest fostered by the recently formed Group Theatre in New York and represented by the work of Sidney Kingsley, Clifford Odets, Maxwell Anderson and Irwin Shaw. In 1936 the Mummers produced Williams's *Headlines*, a curtain-raiser for Irwin Shaw's anti-war drama *Bury the Dead*. In 1937 they produced *Candles to the Sun* and *The Fugitive Kind*, Williams's first two full-length plays, and written – like *Headlines* – in the vein of social protest.

In 1936 Williams enrolled at Washington University, St Louis, where he soon made friends with the campus poet Clark Mills McBurney. The two undergraduates set up what they called 'the literary factory' in the cellar of McBurney's house to write and read together. Williams was studying authors who were to influence his mind and art: Lorca, Melville, Rilke, Rimbaud, and, in particular, Chekhov, D. H. Lawrence and Hart Crane. In the same year Margaret Mitchell's *Gone with the Wind* was published, and Erskine Caldwell, a fellow Southerner, was represented on Broadway by the longest run of the 1930s, *Tobacco Road*.

The pains of early adulthood had been much the same for Williams and his sister until this time. Rose was also put into the business world by C. C. She too, having been disappointed in love, suffered a nervous breakdown and was hospitalised. But, unlike her more fortunate brother, she found no salvation in work. More and more helpless and withdrawn, she was diagnosed a schizophrenic and hospitalised for a second time. In 1937 she was subjected to a pre-frontal lobotomy. She has lived the rest of her life in a sanitarium. The news of the lobotomy came to Williams as a shock from which he never fully recovered. He had been away at the State University of Iowa for his senior year and did not learn of the operation until after it had been performed. Years later he built a shrine in his home in Key West honouring Rose and dedicated to St Jude, patron of lost causes.

Williams received his BA from Iowa in 1938 at the age of twenty-seven and set out on his own. He lived in a boarding-house in the old quarter of New Orleans, a city whose faded antebellum elegance and Bohemian freedom provided the perfect backdrop for his inner development as well as the setting for much of his work. It was during his postgraduate days in New Orleans, recalled in *Vieux Carré*, that he came out as a homosexual and turned himself into a disciplined writer. Early in 1939 he won a prize in a Group Theatre contest for full-length plays by authors not over twenty-five. He had lied about his age to qualify and had entered three one-act dramas – *Moony's Kid Don't Cry*, *The Dark Room*, and *The Case of the Crushed Petunias* – under the title of *American Blues*. The judging-committee was so impressed by the short plays that it awarded him a special prize of $100.

The judges were Irwin Shaw (for whose *Bury the Dead* Williams had written the curtain-raiser *Headlines*), Harold Clurman (who would later direct the Broadway production of *Orpheus Descending*), and Molly Day Thacher (who was to become the wife of Elia Kazan). The most useful contact to arise from the contest was the literary agent Audrey Wood, who for the next thirty years would serve as Williams's manager, banker, adviser and friend. Under her tutelage, he published his short story 'The Field of Blue Children' in *Story* during the summer and by the end of the year had obtained a $1000 Rockefeller grant.

Thomas Lanier Williams III became Tennessee Williams in 1939. 'The Field of Blue Children', which has for its theme a life-determining choice, is the first publication to bear his pen name. He said that he was sometimes called 'Tennessee' in college, that his real name sounded too much like an old-fashioned poet's, and – perhaps most significant – that the life of a writer in America was like that of the Indian fighters of Tennessee among whom he numbered his paternal ancestors. As a child, he had adored the female members of his family and hated his father; but his attitude changed in analysis years later when he came to feel that he owed to his father the fighting blood without which he would not have survived.

Early in 1940 he went to New York, where he enrolled in John Gassner's playwriting workshop at the New School. Gassner, who at the time was also a reader for the Theatre Guild, recommended a full-length play by his new student. The result was the fiasco of *Battle of Angels* in the winter of the same year. The script, later rewritten as *Orpheus Descending*, was an academic exercise in which the young Williams, who still had seen very little professional theatre, put all his dramatic wares on display, mixing heavy-handed symbolism with naturalistic low life in the story of a youthful wayfarer who comes to a small Southern town, where he arouses the interest of the passionate women and the wrath of the envious men. In the climactic fire scene a nervous stage crew, having failed to provide enough smoke from the pots for the dress rehearsal, made up for it by overdoing the effect for the Boston opening. Those in the front rows who had not already left in annoyance with the play did so in greater irritation during the curtain calls, coughing all the way up the aisles and out of the theatre. The production did not come to New York.

The war years mark a low period in Williams's fortunes. Having been rejected for military service because of his weak heart, he drifted from New York to Provincetown, Macon, Jacksonville, New Orleans and St Louis,

14

supporting himself as an elevator-operator, a teletype-operator, waiter, restaurant cashier and movie usher. He had the first of four cataract operations. At the age of thirty-two, he was working as an usher at the Strand Theatre in New York during the first run of *Casablanca* when Audrey Wood called to say that she had negotiated a contract for him as a script-writer at MGM. His weekly salary jumped from $17 to $250; but Williams, unable to bring himself to write dialogue on assignment for screen stars, lasted no more than a few weeks at the studio.

As his contract stipulated that he had to be paid for a minimum of six months, he took the opportunity to write an original screenplay based on his short story 'Portrait of a Girl in Glass'. He sent it to MGM under the title of *The Gentleman Caller* with a note declaring it would outdo *Gone with the Wind*. MGM turned it down. But his spirits were buoyed by his inclusion in James Laughlin's anthology *Five Young American Poets* (1944) and a citation from the American Academy of Arts and Letters. He rewrote the film script as a stage play and sent it to Audrey Wood under a new title, *The Glass Menagerie*. The result was the celebrated production in which Laurette Taylor reached the climax of her career in the role of Amanda Wingfield. When Miss Edwina went backstage after the Chicago opening in 1944, the actress asked, 'And how do you like yourself on the stage?' Miss Edwina denied that there was any resemblance between Amanda and herself beyond a mutual enthusiasm for jonquils. Williams signed over half the rights of the play to her. The quasi-autobiographical drama, about a wandering writer who looks back on the mother and sister he left behind, brought a new voice into the American theatre.

The original Broadway production of *A Streetcar Named Desire* (1947) established Williams as the leading dramatist of the Southern Literary Renaissance. It also marked the beginning of his association with Elia Kazan, who in the same year created the Actors Studio chiefly in order to train the kind of actor best suited to play Williams – one epitomised by Marlon Brando in his performance as Stanley Kowalski. Kazan would later direct the film version of *Streetcar* (1951), the original screenplay *Baby Doll* (1956), and the Broadway productions of *Camino Real* (1953), *Cat on a Hot Tin Roof* (1955) and *Sweet Bird of Youth* (1959).

Although it is not immediately obvious, the autobiographical relevance of *Streetcar* is no less than that of *The Glass Menagerie*. The central dramatic encounter between Blanche DuBois and Stanley Kowalski, the faded Southern belle and the rough, poker-playing ex-soldier whose job keeps him on the road much of the time, is a re-enactment of the struggle between Miss Edwina and C. C. to which Williams had been witness since childhood. (His parents finally separated in the year *Streetcar* opened on Broadway.) But Blanche is also a mask for Williams himself. In the light of the *Memoirs*, a book largely given over to accounts of Williams's brief homosexual contacts, some of the vocabulary in *Streetcar* takes on special autobiographical significance. For example, there is Kowalski's contemptuous remark to Blanche and Stella, 'What do you two think you are? A pair of queens?' or Mitch's to Blanche later, 'I was fool enough to believe you was straight' – to which Blanche replies, 'Who told you I wasn't – "straight"?' She has a longer reply in the screen version, one that Williams in fact quotes in his *Memoirs* in the context of a fleeting homosexual relationship: 'What is straight? A line can be straight, or a street, but the human heart, oh, no, it's curved like a road through mountains!' Even Blanche's famous exit line, 'Whoever you are – I have always depended on the kindness of strangers', resonates as a confession by the author of his reluctance to form close relationships for fear of losing them, and his consequent preference for cruising in the gay world.

With *Streetcar* Williams entered his period of greatest productivity and success. There was a new Williams play on Broadway approximately every two years: *Summer and Smoke* (1948), *The Rose Tattoo* (1951), *Camino Real* (1953), *Cat on a Hot Tin Roof* (1955), *Orpheus Descending* (1957), *Sweet Bird of Youth* (1959), *The Night of the Iguana* (1961). The productions made the reputations of the actors Marlon Brando, Ben Gazzara, Paul Newman, Eli Wallach, Maureen Stapleton, Burl Ives, Barbara Bel Geddes, Geraldine Page, Karl Malden, as well as of the directors José Quintero, Margo Jones, Daniel Mann, Frank Corsaro and, above all, of Elia Kazan. Kazan, who had turned over the Actors Studio to Lee Strasberg after its first few years, cast *Camino Real* almost entirely from its membership.

In addition to the plays, Williams was writing poetry and fiction. *One Arm and Other Stories* appeared in 1948, *The Roman Spring of Mrs Stone* (his first novel) in 1950, *Hard Candy* (a second book of short stories) in 1954, and *In the Winter of Cities* (his first collection of poems) in 1956. Much of Williams's work was now also on the screen: *The Glass Menagerie* came out as a movie in 1950, *Streetcar* in 1951, *The Rose Tattoo* in 1955, *Baby Doll* (an original screenplay) in 1956, *Cat on a Hot Tin Roof* in 1958, *Suddenly Last Summer* in 1959, *The Fugitive Kind* (based on *Orpheus Descending*) in 1960, *Summer and Smoke* in 1961, *The Roman Spring of Mrs Stone* in 1961, and *Sweet Bird of Youth* in 1962. Among his followers and friends a group sharing Williams's traits of style or attitude had grown up; it included Donald Windham, William Inge, Carson McCullers, Jane Bowles and Horton Foote.

The days of bitter penury were over. Williams bought property in New Orleans and Key West; took up painting as a hobby; travelled to Europe, Asia, and Africa; and even settled into a long-term homosexual relationship with Frank Merlo, a man he had met in Provincetown in 1948 and to whom he dedicated *The Rose Tattoo*.

In 1955 he began to take drugs. The year marked the death of his grandfather, the Reverend Walter Dakin, later to be commemorated in the character of the old poet Nonno in *The Night of the Iguana*. It was also the year of the original Broadway production of *Cat on a Hot Tin Roof*, a play in which Williams, through the character of Big Daddy, attempts to work out his relationship with his father. When C. C. died in Memphis in 1957, Williams entered psychoanalysis.

During the 1960s the theatre in New York underwent a radical change, reflecting that of the nation as a whole. Looking back with nostalgia fell out of fashion. People were no longer interested in faded belles and wandering poets, the waifs and strays of a mythical Eden. The war in Vietnam had exploded the illusion of American innocence. In the tide of Women's Liberation and Gay Liberation, Williams's plays – which had derived much of their dramatic tension from female dependency and homosexual guilt – began to look dated. Audiences were discovering Brecht, Beckett, Ionesco, Weiss and other European playwrights who required a kind of performer closer to the agile vaudevillian or the platform orator than to the Method actor. Elia Kazan turned to writing novels, as did William Inge. Carson McCullers died in 1967, five years after William Faulkner. Tennessee Williams entered a period of personal depression and professional decline. After the death of Frank Merlo in 1963, only the production of his plays interrupted his isolation. But his new work, such as *The Gnädiges Fräulein* (1966), which sought to keep pace with the black humour of the times, was not successful. Even familiar Williams drama, such as *Kingdom of Earth* (1968), did not do much better. Williams called the sixties his 'Stoned Age', having propped himself up with drugs and alcohol throughout the decade. In 1969 he followed his brother's example by converting to Catholicism, but toward the end of the year suffered the second nervous breakdown of his life and spent the following three months in the psychiatric ward of a St Louis hospital.

The 1970s and early 1980s were a prolongation of restless experiment and commercial failure. The only exception was *Small Craft Warnings* (1972), Williams's first financial success since *The Night of the Iguana* over a decade earlier. To boost sales for the off-Broadway production, he made his professional acting-debut in the role of Doc and sometimes took questions from the audience after the performance. The play is set in a small-town bar on the west coast where lost, anxious, or cynical souls come to confess their unhappy histories. The confessionalist urge in Williams himself, evident from the start, became more pronounced during this period. He published his *Memoirs* in 1975, and in the same year a second novel, *Moise and the World of Reason*, in which he appears under different guises – the young homosexual writer filling his notebooks through the night, the middle-aged dramatist worried about the production of his new play at the Truck and Warehouse Theatre (where *Small Craft Warnings* had been produced a few years beforehand). Three of Williams's late plays are clearly autobiographical. *Vieux Carré* (1977) and *Something Cloudy, Something Clear* (1981) are wistful recollections of youth in New Orleans and Provincetown. *Kirche, Kutchen, und Kinder*, which received its premiere in the same year as the death of Williams's mother (1980), is a spoof at the expense of the playwright himself in the very act of remembering his past.

Williams's lonely death in the winter of 1983 was consistent with his life and art. He had lived as an exile from Eden in a fallen world where his only real solace lay in the power of his words. He died in a run-down hotel with a lobby the size of a kitchen but a name, the Elysée, that winks at paradise. The last address was fitting for the author whose heroine gets off a streetcar at Elysian Fields and resides as a transient in a city far from home until the hour of her final exit.

2
Form, Theme and Character

It is this continual rush of time, so violent that it appears to be screaming, that deprives our actual lives of so much dignity and meaning, and it is, perhaps more than anything else the *arrest of time* which has taken place in a completed work of art that gives to certain plays their feeling of depth and significance.

('The Timeless World of a Play')

Tennessee Williams is perhaps the only genuine *writer* in the history of the American theatre. He published two books of poetry, two novels, four books of short stories (one including a novella), a book of essays, and his *Memoirs*. During his lifetime, at least sixty-three of his plays and playlets (thirty-two are short, twenty-four full-length and seven mid-length) were published or given a major professional production or both. He wrote or collaborated upon seven of the fifteen film adaptations.

One reason for the great similarity in Williams's work is that he constantly recycled his material. *Sweet Bird of*

Youth, Small Craft Warnings and *Camino Real* all began as short plays. The revised version of *Battle of Angels* takes it title from a poem on the same theme, 'Orpheus Descending'. The film adaptation is renamed after an early unpublished play, *The Fugitive Kind. The Eccentricities of a Nightingale* is a revision of *Summer and Smoke*, which itself began as a short story, 'The Yellow Bird'. The screen play *Baby Doll* derives from two short plays, *The Unsatisfactory Supper* and *27 Wagons Full of Cotton. 27 Wagons* had begun as a short story, and *Baby Doll* was in turn rewritten as a stage play, *Tiger Tail.*

Perhaps the fact that most of the full-length plays are expansions of short works, at least half of them short stories, helps to explain why Williams has often been criticised for his weak dramatic structure. As Eric Bentley suggests in *What is Theatre?*, the structure comes out of the modern short story rather than out of the well-made play. The interest is not in plot so much as it is in character, mood and condition. *The Glass Menagerie* (1944), for example, has no Scribean intrigue. Based on the short story 'Portrait of a Girl in Glass', the play is a loosely connected series of scenes which conspire to create the narrator's nostalgic recollection of his family. The climax is not Laura's disappointment with her only gentleman caller but the recognition by Tom that for all the miles he has travelled he has never really broken the tender ties with his mother and his sister. By the same token, *The Two-Character Play* (1967) becomes accessible when seen not as an attempt to tell a sad tale on stage so much as a theatrical exploration of psychic pain. Williams's typical dramatic form, early and late, is not linear but exfoliative, not narrative but lyric, as indeed has been that of the modern short story – including his own – since Joyce's *Dubliners*.

What matters is the working-up to a climactic

illumination of character and circumstances, or as Joyce called it, an 'epiphany'. In Williams's short story 'The Field of Blue Children' a young woman acknowledges the absence of poetry and wonder in her life when she recalls a former relationship. In 'The Vine' an actor just beginning to age comes to recognise his failure and dependency. In the autobiographical 'Angel in the Alcove' the imaginary figure of Williams's grandmother witnesses his deepening loneliness, fear and shame (the story is the nucleus of *Vieux Carré*). In both the full-length play *The Night of the Iguana* and the short story of the same name from which it evolves, the main point is the revelation that comes through trial.

The drama of Tennessee Williams derives its lyric naturalism from the adaptation of the modern short story for the cinematic theatre. Throughout the canon, film techniques undermine the conventions of stage realism. Music comes out of nowhere. Lighting is symbolic. Fragmentary sets and transparent gauze scrims, as George Brandt has so aptly said, minimise the difference between interiors and exteriors, making scene transitions fluid and immediate.[1] Indeed the shooting-script is the idea behind Williams's production notes to *The Glass Menagerie*. The 'new plastic theatre' must make full use of all the resources of the contemporary stage – language, action, scenery, music, costume, sound, lighting – and bind them into an artistic unity conceived by the playwright.

To see a Williams play in performance is to be present at a drama of encounters among essentially naturalistic characters within a frankly evocative setting where reality is interfused with the stuff of dreams. On occasion there is a reasonable excuse for nonrealistic touches. The scenes of *The Glass Menagerie* are entitled to poetic licence because they represent the memories of the narrator. The mysterious voices that whisper from behind the walls toward the end of *Streetcar* are projections of Blanche's insanity. But the fact is that Williams is never a realist in the photographic or journalistic sense, as his directions to the scene-designer indicate:

> The set represents in nonrealistic fashion a general dry-goods store and part of a connecting 'confectionary' in a small Southern town. . . . Merchandise is represented very sparsely and it is not realistic.
>
> *(Orpheus Descending)*

> The scene is a somewhat nonrealistic evocation of a bar on the beach-front in one of those coastal towns between Los Angeles and San Diego. *(Small Craft Warnings)*

> The set may be as unrealistic as the decor of a dramatic ballet. *(Suddenly Last Summer)*

> The set should be far less realistic than I have so far implied in this description of it. I think the walls below the ceiling should dissolve mysteriously into air; the set should be roofed by the sky; stars and moon suggested by traces of milky pallor, as if they were observed through a telescope lens out of focus. *(Cat on a Hot Tin Roof)*

Williams plans his sets, costumes, and lighting with a painter's eye. The poker-players in *Streetcar*, he writes, must be costumed in the lurid colours of Van Gogh. The lighting in *The Glass Menagerie* should take its cue, not from reality, but from El Greco. Allegorical names (Chance Wayne, Valentine Xavier, Flora Goforth) frequently match the non-realistic visual effects, and even the actors are sometimes directed to deliver their lines in a non-realistic way:

24

The evenly cadenced lines of the dialogue between Baby Doll and Archie Lee may be given a singsong reading, somewhat like a grotesque choral incantation, and passages may be divided as strophe and antistrophe by Baby Doll's movements back and forth on the porch.

(*The Unsatisfactory Supper*)

Mandolin begins to fade in. The following monologue should be treated frankly as exposition, spoken to the audience, almost directly, with a force that commands attention. Dolly does not remain in the playing area, and after the first few sentences, there is no longer any pretense of a duologue. (*Orpheus Descending*)

Williams's lyricism is not simply a matter of words, as his comprehensive use of the non-verbal elements of playmaking shows. He is not a poet in the theatre but a theatre poet. His actual poetry, written for the most part in a loose and prosaic free verse, rarely exploits to advantage either the metaphoric or the musical resources of language. It is true, however, that the outstanding literary quality of his drama is in the dialogue that he creates out of the natural poetry of Southern American speech, an idiom that is at once rhythmical, imagistic and genuine. Still, it is painful to imagine how much would be lost in a radio version of *Streetcar*.[2]

Consider, for example, the most famous line in the play, if not in all Williams: 'Whoever you are – I have always depended on the kindness of strangers'. Torn from its theatrical context, it is hardly 'poetic'. But in performance it is unforgettable. Blanche DuBois – widowed, jobless, evicted, raped by her brother-in-law, committed by her sister, thinking that perhaps her old beau has come for her

25

but alarmed instead to see the grim nurse and the doctor from the asylum, the men in the next room at the table for poker, the pathetic paper lantern she had bought to cover the naked light bulb pulled off and thrust toward her by Kowalski as he had earlier thrust toward her a one-way ticket back to Laurel as a 'birthday present', admonitions echoing from the walls around her like threatening shadows – the deranged and frightened Blanche, despite her tears and screams, is now pinned to the floor by the nurse who asks the doctor whether to get a straitjacket. When out of this violence and torment the doctor calls her 'Miss DuBois', says the jacket is not necessary, makes the nurse let go, raises Blanche to her feet, removes his hat and offers his arm, she responds by smiling up at him as she would 'at a new beau', looking triumphantly at the nurse and back at the doctor again while the rest of the stage is still, and then, having crossed up centre and adjusted her hood, she turns to her escort in the doorway and says, 'Whoever you are – I have always depended on the kindness of strangers', and goes out with him to the car that will take her to the asylum, as Stanley comforts Stella, the closing music comes up, the poker game resumes, and the curtain slowly falls. The exit line, resonant with the plight of Blanche, hangs in the air for long afterwards.

It defines the essential Williams condition: that of a sensitive creature who has no home in an alien world. That is why evictions, banishments, or the loss of a cherished place of refuge – threatened or actual – are so frequent in Williams's plays (*Streetcar, Orpheus, Cat, Kingdom of Earth, Gnädiges Fräulein, This Property is Condemned*). They are a theatrical metaphor of alienation. The lost home may not always be a real one, like the ancestral estate of the DuBois family. In fact, more often it is simply the beautiful dream for which Belle Reve is primarily a symbol.

It is the enchanted time of youth, love, beauty, gentility and innocence.

Time seen in its elegiac aspect as a dimension of decay is the great Williams theme. The brief period of bloom exists only as a reverie. The scenic correlative of this point of view is in the frequent opposition of two areas in a Williams setting. The interior of the Wingfield apartment in *Menagerie*, and especially of the living-room where Laura plays her old records and polishes her glass figurines, contrasts with the grim exterior of the tenement with its adjacent alleys and fire escapes. In *Orpheus* the 'confectionary' that Lady Torrance has made to resurrect the lost wine garden of her father contrasts with the Gothic ugliness of the mercantile store and the town surrounding it. In *Kingdom of Earth* the parlour with its chandelier and golden chairs where Lot dies dressed in his dead mother's clothes contrasts with the farmhouse kitchen in which most of the action occurs. All three dim poetic interiors are characterised by fragile glass – animal figurines, chandelier pendants, tree ornaments and wind chimes.

Nearly all of Williams's plays are, like *Menagerie*, 'memory plays'. They look back with longing to a time that has been sweetened in the remembering. The pathos of life consists in the heedless trampling over precious moments by the blind rush of events. That is why the festive occasion so often occurs in Williams as a metaphor of the attempt to recapture in the present what has been lost in the past. Annual celebrations, which rest upon a cyclical rather than a linear sense of time, and seek to hold golden hours within a kind of magical parenthesis, are always ruined in Williams's plays: birthdays (*Streetcar*, *Cat*), Easter (*Sweet Bird*, *Orpheus*), Christmas (*Mutilated*, *Period of Adjustment*, *Moony's Kid*), Independence Day (*Summer and Smoke*). The ruined festive occasion is the abrupt denial of the enchanted time of holiday by the brutal reality of everyday. It corresponds to the extinction of the poetic interior after Laura blows out her candles, Lot dies, or Lady's confectionary fails to open (significantly, on the day before Easter). It is like an interrupted performance or the early closing of a play. Indeed, the spoiled occasion is sometimes an unsatisfactory presentation (*Two-Character Play, The Gnädiges Fräulein, Lord Byron's Love Letter*) or simply an unsuccessful dinner (*Menagerie, Unsatisfactory Supper*). The hope and imagination that engender the special time, place or event suggest the artist's effort to create beauty in the face of inevitable change. But then art too in Williams is usually seen in pitiful terms: Val Xavier's book in *Battle*, Sebastian Venable's poem a year in *Suddenly*, Christopher Flanders's mobiles in *Milk Train*, Mark Conley's painting in *Tokyo Hotel*, Zelda Fitzgerald's dancing in *Clothes*.

The very titles of Williams's works, with their frequent reference to vehicles or journeys, warm seasons and passing days, suggest metaphors of transience: *Summer and Smoke, Suddenly Last Summer, Clothes for a Summer Hotel, The Roman Spring of Mrs Stone, A Lovely Sunday for Creve Coeur, The Night of the Iguana, Period of Adjustment, Small Craft Warnings, The Milk Train Doesn't Stop Here Anymore, A Streetcar Named Desire, Camino Real*. The face of time is always that of the destroyer, never the healer. Hence, the elegiac strain runs through Williams in the continual re-enactment of loss. Life succumbs to death, youth to age, the yearning spirit to the waning flesh, gentility to brutality, beneficient nature to crass commercialism, goodness to corruption, and even the energy of art to the passion in the world for 'declivity'.

These themes dominate Williams's two collections of poems, *In the Winter of Cities* (1964) and *Androgyne, Mon*

Amour (1977). The elegiac strain is not only in the requiems themselves, such as 'Cortege' or 'A Wreath for Alexandra Molostvova'. It is also in 'The Harp of Wales', in which the poet pays tribute to the instrument made for keening 'the deaths of the wild gray kings'; and runs through all the poems about loneliness in age – 'Lonesome Man', 'Old Men with Sticks', 'Old Men are Fond', and 'Old Men Go Mad at Night'. It recurs in 'The Lady with No One at All' when, in an action reminiscent of *Streetcar* after Blanche has been stood up by Mitch, 'Milady' turns before a cracked pier mirror in a dim hallway to appraise the wisp of lilac chiffon she has just thrown over her shoulders, and then imagines that she is out in a boat on a pond large as a lake with the man she lost long ago. *Streetcar* also lurks behind the plaintive 'Lament for the Moths', which mourns the disappearance from a mammoth-haunted world of the fragile nocturnal creatures to which Williams likens his most famous heroine. 'Orpheus Descending' pictures the under kingdom as a place where light cannot enter and movement is barely possible. To this end the poet and singer must learn that for all his gifts he shall surely come. The theme of art's defeat is also in the references in 'Mornings on Bourbon Street' to the would-be writer who died at sea and the would-be painter who earned her living as a prostitute, two among the former companions for which the speaker weeps as he recalls the loss of his youth, of his innocence, and of his belief in the ability to love.

The elegiac persona of nearly all Williams's lyrics proliferates into the many characters throughout his fiction who are victims of time. It is because Williams sees life as a brief bloom and long decay that he specialises in portraits of men and women during their transition from the aspiration of youth to the disappointment of age. Death, failure and loneliness intermittently relieved by guilty sex are the constants in the author's view of the human condition.

Four short stories from Williams's first collection, *One Arm and Other Stories* (1948), end in the suicide, execution or fatal exhaustion of men still young. The hero of 'One Arm' is Oliver Winemiller, an ex-navy boxer with the looks of Apollo who became an itinerant homosexual prostitute after losing his arm in a car accident. Now awaiting electrocution for the drunken murder of a wealthy broker who had wanted him to perform in a blue movie, he receives letters of gratitude and confession from former clients who regard him as their saviour. Even the young Lutheran minister who visits the prison leaves deeply shaken by his own repressed sexuality in the presence of the condemned Oliver. The title character of 'The Poet' is a tall blond man of sculpturesque good looks, a kind of evangelist, poet–prophet, story-teller and maker of spectacles, who is used sexually by grateful strangers as he sleeps in alleyways during his wanderings. He dies on a beach after a final creative effort among the young adolescents who make up his audience of followers.

The death of a very different kind of wanderer occurs in 'The Malediction'. The hero is a panicky little man with a prematurely old face (Lucio) who has been living as a transient in a Northern industrial city and submitting to sex with his aggressive landlady. A drunken beggar, declaring himself to be God, curses the sins of the world. Lucio, having lost his job at the factory, drowns himself with the wounded cat that had been his only solace. The story is dramatised as the early one-act *Strangest Kind of Romance*. The hero of 'Desire and the Black Masseur' is another painfully repressed little man (Anthony Burns), who at the age of thirty still has the unformed look of a child. He fulfils his sexual desire by being pummelled, broken and devoured by a huge black masseur during the Lenten season while in a nearby church a preacher exhorts the congregation to atone.

Anthony Burns is only the most grotesque example of the hero-as-scapegoat in Williams's fiction. Oliver Winemiller is a 'saviour' to the many who bought and sold him, the evangelical 'poet' dies preaching the word, and even the unfortunate Lucio casts light on man's inhumanity by his love for the homeless cat with whom he drowns. A melancholy combination of death, desire and religiosity hangs over these four stories, whose sexually passive heroes are sacrificial figures in a fallen world and haunted fugitives from its brutal reality.

A gentler treatment of the destructive experience of human life occurs in Williams's first novel, *The Roman Spring of Mrs Stone* (1950), a work which provides the major example of the faded belle in his fiction. The 1961 screen adaptation was written by Gavin Lambert and directed by José Quintero with Vivien Leigh as Karen and Warren Beatty as Paolo. The rich, widowed, once beautiful Karen Stone, now in her menopause, having retired from the stage after bad reviews in a role for which she had grown too old, goes to Rome, where she forms an attachment with a vain and handsome gigolo (Paolo). When at the end he leaves her for another customer, she succumbs to the lewd advances of a young street Arab. The fall of Mrs Stone from fame to degradation is seen against the backdrop of the warm Italian spring. Born to privilege in the South, flattered in her prime, she is dependent in her age 'on the kindness of strangers'. Time's decay is again the subject of this typical Williams work whose easeful elegiac mood permeates its vision of youth lost and beauty faded within the ruined grandeur of the ancient capital of empire.

Rome as a metaphor of Williams's elegiac view of life is

continuous with New Orleans as well as with the Joy Rio, the once elegant opera house, now a third-rate cinema, which provides the setting for two stories from his second collection of short fiction, *Hard Candy: A Book of Stories* (1954). In both the title work and 'The Mysteries of the Joy Rio' a homosexual, one old and the other early middle-aged, succumbs to a fatal illness while in pursuit of a fleeting encounter in the upper reaches of the old theatre. The first is a retired candy merchant of seventy who is found dead of thrombosis between two chairs in one of the tiny boxes that still extend in tiers of golden chains from one side of the great proscenium to the other. The second is a forty-year-old watch-repairman who, in a delirium resulting from the final stage of terminal cancer, imagines that he meets his long-dead lover and benefactor on the great marble staircase that leads from the first balcony to the tiers above, roped off for the past twenty years, into whose Stygian blackness he has fled from an abusive usher. The sallow little moon-faced hero at forty looks no older than he suddenly did at twenty-five after the death of the older man from whom he had learned the mysteries of the place that became his secret pleasure.

The constant pursuit of furtive sex recurs in 'Two on a Party', a picaresque story from the same collection in which Bill and Cora, a homosexual Southern writer *manqué* and a disinherited Louisiana belle, both beginning to age, earn a living by working together as itinerant prostitutes. Fading appeal and artistic failure are also central to the portrait of Donald, the unemployed early middle-aged actor of 'The Vine', who spends his day wandering about town in the futile hope of finding someone to restore his ebbing confidence. Both stories focus on sorry fugitives from time.

Variations on the idea of a once-handsome drifter of about thirty with disappointed artistic or aesthetic inclinations appear in Williams's third collection of short fiction, *The Knightly Quest: A Novella and Four Stories* (1966). In 'Man Bring This Up Road' a thirty-four-year-old failed poet and mobile sculptor, finding himself penniless abroad, appeals for help to a wealthy seventy-two-year-old woman who turns him down (the story is the basis of *The Milk Train Doesn't Stop Here Anymore*). In 'Mama's Old Stucco House' a young failed painter returns from New York to Macon at the time of his mother's death and devotes his time to seeking homosexual encounters at the neighbouring air base. *The Knightly Quest* is a comic fantasy whose hero, the aesthetic homosexual son of an aristocratic Southern family (Gewinner Pearce), returns from abroad to find that the small town he grew up in has turned into an industrial city dedicated to manufacturing an ultimate weapon of destruction. He blows up his brother's factory and escapes from earth in a space ship. The novella's title refers to Gewinner's nocturnal cruising as well as to his quixotic crusade against war and commerce. Ultimately, it also alludes to his longing for a place, like the region of weightless ozone through which the space ship at the end is said to be flying, where there is neither day nor night, watches are set to light-years, and the sorrows of lost time are left far behind.

Analogous variations on the idea of the faded belle, ranging from the pathetic to the farcical, appear in William's fourth book of short stories. Its collection title, *Eight Mortal Ladies Possessed* (1974), defines the leading characters as well-bred, passionate women subject to time's decay. In 'Sabbatha and Solitude', a poetess, celebrated in her youth, would now die of loneliness without her young lover. In 'Completed', a painfully shy nineteen-year-old withdraws after her first experience of menstruation to spend the rest of her life as a recluse. In

'The Inventory at Fontana Bella', a 102-year-old *principessa*, five times married, has one last gaudy night before she expires. In 'Happy August the Tenth', a woman from an old Virginia family confronts the onslaught of middle age with her lesbian lover as she looks out from their New York apartment in early morning upon 'the illuminated tombstones' of 'the world's biggest necropolis'.

Williams's short stories are elegiac character sketches within narrative frames. Of the twenty-eight in his four collections, fourteen end in death, six in climactic self-discoveries, and two in both. Oliver Winemiller sees himself in a new light before his execution and Anthony Burns comes to realise that what he has been seeking is to die in just the way he does. Rosemary McCool could be added to this group, the heroine of 'Completed', who chooses a kind of death-in-life following the shocking realisation of her womanhood. Even among the remaining seven stories there is almost always an image of impending mortality as in 'Happy August the Tenth', an awareness of decline as in 'Man Bring This Up Road', or a sense, as in 'Two on a Party', that the flight from time is a loser's game.

Like his fiction, Williams's drama presents human beings as victims of time. The plays are filled with the outcasts of life: the old, the bereft, the mutilated, the tormented, the lovelorn, the homeless and the forgotten. As in the stories, two main character types – the faded belle and the wanderer – stand out from the rest as if to illustrate time's most pathetic casualties: the has-been and the might-have-been. The wanderer receives his definitive portrait as Valentine Xavier in *Orpheus*, the faded belle hers as Blanche DuBois in *Streetcar*. Both are present in Williams's essential and quasi-autobiographical play, *The Glass Menagerie*. Amanda and Laura Wingfield, mother and daughter, one an anachronism and the other a recluse, are only two of the many incarnations of the faded belle which are Williams's hallmark – colourful butterflies transformed by cruel time into grey moths. Tom Wingfield, the son, an aspiring writer who joins the merchant marine, is only one in a long line of wanderers – handsome young men with 'the charm of the defeated', just past their youth, nursing disappointed ideals or fragile artistic hopes as they move aimlessly through dangerous country.

It may be useful at this point to step back from the two archetypal characters to see what their essential stories are. In the story of the wanderer, a good-looking young man (1) from the South and (2) of sensitive nature, (3) sometimes with a name that suggests his divine origin, (4) leaves home to become an itinerant artist of some sort, until, (5) just past his youth and (6) tainted with sexual corruption but still (7) pure of heart, (8) he attaches himself to an older woman (9) of property and station (10) to whom he brings comfort before he (11) submits to violent punishment (12) at the hands of a group of angry male figures. In the story of the faded belle, an attractive young woman (1) of sensitive nature, (2) born in the South (3) of good or even of aristocratic family, and having (4) a refinement of taste and sensibility and (5) a puritanical fastidiousness about sex, (6) is disappointed in love at an early age, and as a result (7) either ends her life as a recluse or (8) abandons herself to promiscuity, (9) especially with younger men, (10) but in either case probably becomes deranged, and, (11) after losing her youth, her looks, and sometimes even a home of her own, (12) is taken away to an institution.

These two remarkably similar stories, or versions of them, or bits and pieces of them, run through the dramatic canon from beginning to end. They also sometimes interweave. For example, the older woman to whom the wanderer attaches himself partakes of the unhappy faded belle (Lady Torrance, Alexandra Del Lago, Violet Venable, Flora Goforth). Similarly, the younger man with whom the faded belle has a fleeting relationship late in her career bears a resemblance to the lonely, suppliant wanderer (the inexperienced travelling salesman at the end of *Summer and Smoke*, the needy street Arab in *Mrs Stone*, the Young Collector for the evening paper in *Streetcar*).

Both archetypes are masks of Tennessee Williams. The wanderer is the struggling author as a lonely young man with a classic Oedipal fixation. The violence he submits to after his relationship with an older woman shows his dread of paternal vengeance for having sex with his mother. The faded belle at first looks like Rose and Miss Edwina. Seen in perspective, however, she is the homosexual playwright as a neurasthenic female with a fear of losing out in middle age. There is usually something theatrical about the belle, a something whose day is passed, or that comes to naught, or that was never much to begin with. Alma Winemiller, Karen Stone, Alexandra Del Lago, Flora Goforth and the Gnädiges Fräulein are, or were, all performers. Lady Torrance shows her creativity in the design of a 'confectionary' that does not open. The production Amanda Wingfield makes of the evening Jim O'Connor calls is a flop. Nor does the eloquent Blanche DuBois, English-teacher and poet's widow, make a hit with the groundling, Kowalski, by playing the lady.

The frequent encounter of the belle and the wanderer as lovers within the same play appears to support Freud's notion that homosexuality proceeds from a narcissistic basis. Seen in this light, the plays are fantasies in which Williams, identifying with his mother, finds a partner resembling himself to love as his mother loved him. But sex rarely offers more than a temporary respite from loneliness in Williams. Nor does art have charm to soothe the savage breast. Their failure in the face of time's inexorable decay is the common condition of his two personal myths. The artistic inadequacy of the archetypal figures is continuous with the 'poetry' of their speech. Their intellectual level is on a par with that of the culture club over which Alma Winemiller presides, the chapter of the Daughters of the American Revolution to which Amanda Wingfield belongs, or the high-school English classes that Blanche DuBois has taught in rural Mississippi. Their stale imagery is analogous to the costume jewellery and summer furs that the one-time heiress of Belle Reve carries in her trunk, the paper lantern with which she covers the naked light bulb, or the slipcovers, pillows and fan with which she decorates the squalid Kowalski apartment. In *Dialogue in American Drama*, Ruby Cohn has shown that, despite its syntax and vocabulary, Blanche's language is marked by trite expressions and incongruous comparisons that reflect her weak imagination. When Stanley says, 'What poetry!' in response to Blanche's hope that the eyes of Stella's baby will be like two blue candles in a white cake, we can only agree. Williams gives his faded belles not a poetry, but a gushiness of speech. His wanderers, such as Val Xavier, Chance Wayne and Tom Wingfield, are even more poignant because they combine forced imagery with the quest for Significance.

Nevertheless, the haunting quality of Williams's best work is rooted in his poetic temperament. He was an essentially private man who fought hard to become a public one in order to achieve success in the collaborative enterprise of theatre. His struggle to overcome the fear of exposure is evident in the frequency with which his characters create spectacles of themselves. Their need of attention prompts them to choose words and to make scenes for which they are punished by contempt or disregard. As figments of their author's paranoia, they are poor players whose script is no stronger than their performance in the hopeless contest of imagination with hard fact or of fond memory with present pain. As victims of time, they are sensitive creatures, trapped in the here and now, seeking escape into the there and then. One flees aimlessly across the face of earth, a homeless sojourner on a forever-alien planet. The other seeks refuge as a recluse or a mental patient within the secrecy of her own frightened heart. The vain effort to bring lasting beauty into a changing, heedless world enacts the playwright's own endeavour and reflects his sombre view. The faded belle and the wanderer, the has-been and the might-have-been, are elegiac characters of 'the fugitive kind' and still-born poets whose muffled outcries are destined to oblivion by the tyranny of time.

3
Early One-Act Plays
(1939—46)

CHARLIE COLTON. My pockets are full of watches that
tell me my time's just about over. (*The Last of my
Solid Gold Watches*)

Tennessee Williams was an artist most at home in the short
form. His poems are all short, nearly all his fiction is as
well, and as a matter of fact most of his plays are too. But
the short play is not a viable commercial length – a fact
which makes the dating of the early one-act plays
problematic. Of those discussed in this chapter, most were
written by 1939 and all by 1946, but only a few have ever
been seen either on or off Broadway. To meet the demands
of convention for full-length plays, Williams had to adapt,
or to combine, or to expand his short works. Yet, although
he learned to broaden his canvas, he remained a quick-
sketch artist at heart. That is why his early one-acters not
only provide an index to his career but also include some of
his finest achievements.[1]

They fall into two groups. The first group, cast in

Williams's characteristic mode of lyric naturalism, is comprised of a gallery of miniature portraits of the faded belle. The second group is more heterogeneous. The majority of plays are sketches of the wanderer, or of young men who resemble him in some significant respects; but a few plays centre on neither of Williams's two main archetypes. The mode varies from verse to prosaic realism; it shows Williams in his late twenties moving away from the social protest of the Group Theatre, whose era preceded his own, and closer to the confessional content of his emerging elegiac drama.

1. Sketches of the faded belle

It was on the strength of her performance as Lucretia Collins in the Los Angeles Actors Laboratory production of *Portrait of a Madonna* in 1947 that Jessica Tandy was cast to play Blanche DuBois in the original Broadway production of *Streetcar* later in the same year. Lucretia is a faded Southern belle who has been living as a recluse in a Northern-city apartment unable to forget the man she loved and lost in her youth. She now imagines that after all these years he has found his way back to her, somehow stolen into her room, and made her pregnant.

The removal of the psychotic heroine to an asylum by a doctor and nurse at the end of the play is, so to speak, a first draft of the last scene of *Streetcar*. Lucretia's similarity to Alma Winemiller is perhaps even more striking. Both women are raised in the shadow of the Episcopal church and both rebel. Indeed their fathers were both ministers in Glorious Hill, where Lucretia, like Alma in *The Eccentricities of a Nightingale*, the revision of *Summer and Smoke*, had taught the primary class at Sunday school and made the costumes for the Christmas pageant. Both lose the men they love to more aggressive rivals. The uninhibited Nellie Ewell, who takes John Buchanan away from Alma, is foreshadowed by the 'shameless' Evelyn, who disappears from the picnic with Richard Martin and does not return with him until dark. At the end of *Summer and Smoke* Alma turns to casual sex. At the end of *Madonna* Lucretia vows that she will educate her child privately to protect him from the 'evil' influence of her church.

The rejection of Christian schooling by the heroine of a play whose title associates her with the holy virgin is one part of the central dramatic irony. Instead of the beautiful Mary, mother of Jesus, made pregnant by the spirit of God, Williams's madonna is a middle-aged spinster with hunched back and desiccated face, who in her derangement believes she has been made to conceive by rape. The additional irony of her association with the Lucretia of Roman legend lies in the contrast between the model of matronly virtue who committed suicide after being raped, and the faded belle who persists in the pathetic efforts at allurement evident in her corkscrew curls and old-fashioned négligé.

Frank, the 'smarty pants' of an elevator boy, opposes Lucretia's wishful delusion with harsh reality. He ridicules her for thinking that a man would climb up the building to enter her room, makes fun of her cherished picture of Richard Martin, and is even prepared to steal some of her old phonograph records as 'curiosities' for his girlfriend. In his lack of comprehension, his normal sexual vigour, his vulgarity and his mocking sense of humour, Frank is to Lucretia the beginning of what Stanley is to Blanche.

Whereas Blanche and Alma try to get past their pain, Lucretia treasures hers. Alma takes up with strangers;

Blanche, after doing so too, is later willing to settle for marriage with Mitch; but Lucretia is locked within her role as lovelorn maiden, a case of arrested development at a point of significant loss. Her only solution, finally – it is of course Blanche's as well – is the escape into merciful insanity. With Richard's picture, taken on the day of the terrible picnic, placed on the mantle, her clothes and furniture unchanged since she left Glorious Hill, she has played the same sad story, like the music of an old record, over and over again until, so to speak, the record broke.

The phonograph in Miss Collins's apartment serves both a symbolic and a practical purpose. The porter puts on a record of 'I'm Forever Blowing Bubbles' while he and the elevator boy wait for Miss Collins to enter. The thematic relevance of the old waltz is the same as that of 'It's Only a Paper Moon', which Blanche sings in *Streetcar*. Both songs allude to the creation of beauty out of ordinary things, the charm of illusion, and the idea of make-believe which is the basis of theatre. Both heroines are sensitive creatures bewildered by loss, living under sentence of decay.

Like Lucretia Collins, the Old Woman in *Lord Byron's Love Letter* is a faded belle whose lost love marks the boundaries of her life. She and her companion, a middle-aged spinster, eke out a living in late-nineteenth-century New Orleans by showing tourists a letter said to have been written by Lord Byron to the spinster's grandmother, Irénée Marguerite de Poitevent.[2] The curtain line discloses that the old woman is herself the once-beautiful sixteen-year-old Irénée, who recorded in her travel journal, part of which is read to the tourists, how she met a handsome young man with a barely perceptible limp on the steps of the Acropolis and fell in love nearly three quarters of a century ago.

The gaps and inaccuracies of the story make it uncertain

whether the man was Byron, or, if he was, whether he had an affair with Irénée, or, if he did, whether the spinster Ariadne is his granddaughter. Byron, who died in 1824, could not have been climbing the steps of the Acropolis in 1827, the year Irénée says they met. Nor did he die 'in action' or 'in battle' as the two women tell the tourists, but of a fever in Missolonghi. Neither was it Byron who 'burned the body of the poet Shelley', although it is true that he was present at the cremation. The theatrical cliché by which Irénée says she met Byron – she dropped her glove and he returned it – suggests a high-strung girl's romantic fabrication. What happened next between the man on the steps, whoever he may have been, and the 'faint' and 'breathless' Southern belle we can only guess, because the old woman stops the spinster's reading at that crucial point in the journal. Most teasing of all, the climax of the presentation – the great man's love letter itself – the tourists are permitted to view from a distance but not to read.

Still, Irénée is old now and might be confused about dates and details. Her declaration that Byron was killed in action could be an understandable exaggeration. He did devote the last period of his life to helping the Greeks in their war of independence against the Turks. The letter, if it was written by Byron in love, would be the most private document in her possession. The truth about Byron and Irénée therefore lies hidden. Perhaps she did meet him and have a child by him who was one of Ariadne's parents. Perhaps she never met him, and the letter is a hoax – in which case the comic tourists, Mr and Mrs Winston Tutwiler of Milwaukee, who dash off at the end without paying, conclude the play's action with a classic tit-for-tat.

Like Henry James's *Aspern Papers*, which it echoes, *Lord Byron's Love Letter* will not yield its secret. But, whatever the case, it is clear that something happened to Irénée long ago in Athens, a brief, intensely romantic experience – whether real, or imaginary, or both – and that after it was over she became a recluse living only in its memory. Behind the lines of her sonnet to Byron – quoted below without the interruptions contained in the play – appears to lurk the shadowy story of an unforgotten summer romance:

> *Un saison enchanté*! [sic] I mused. Beguiled
> Seemed Time herself, her erstwhile errant ways
> Briefly forgotten, she stayed here and smiled
> Caught in a net of gold and azure days.
> But I lacked wit to see how lightly shoon
> Were Time and you, to vagrancy so used
> That by the touch of one October moon
> From summer's tranquil spell you might be loosed!
> Think you love is writ on my soul with chalk,
> To be washed off with a few parting tears?
> Then you know not with what slow steps I walk
> The barren way of those hibernal years –
> My life a vanished interlude, a shell
> Whose walls are your first kiss – and last farewell!

As Blanche DuBois would say about her own first love, the searchlight that had been turned on the world was suddenly turned off, and since then no light has been stronger than that of a kitchen candle.

For that matter, Byron, who corresponds to the likewise unseen Richard Martin in *Madonna* as the man the heroine loved and lost, bears a strong resemblance to Blanche's dead husband. He conforms to Williams's archetypal wanderer – the doomed, idealistic and handsome artist just past youth, his background steeped in sexual scandal.

Whatever else may lie behind this little play, it presents an early encounter of the wanderer and the faded belle.

Irénée and Ariadne anticipate the mother and daughter in *Menagerie* as two lonely women bereft of support, the one with memories of an exciting past, the other never having bloomed. But memory serves a different purpose in the one-act play, which gives a composite picture of the belle at three stages of time. She is at once the obedient middle-aged spinster reading to the tourists, the adolescent Irénée whose journal provides their entertainment, and the old woman who directs the proceedings from behind a curtain, one claw-like hand all that is visible. Seeing through the lens of the past into a still more remote past in *Lord Byron's Love Letter* is like containing memory within memory in *The Glass Menagerie*. Set a century ago, the play reveals how an old woman who had grown up during the age of Romanticism responded to what seemed to her an ideal world. The Southern belle saw ancient Greece through the eyes of the poets when she set forth in Athens in the bloom of her youth.

The enchanted summer of Irénée Marguerite de Poitevent is enshrined in her literary efforts. But the cherished past cannot withstand the vulgar onslaught of hibernal days. The humiliating reality of age disrupts the *belle rêve* of youth. The pathetic attempt to arrest time, to hold forever love's young dream, has turned the belle into an embittered old crone reduced to selling precious memories to strangers.

A contrapuntal stage direction follows the recitation of the sonnet to Byron: 'The band, leading the parade, has started down the street, growing rapidly louder. It passes by like the heedless, turbulent years. The Husband, roused from his stupor, lunges to the door.' Having slept through the resurrection of Irénée's love affair, the tipsy, cigar-smoking Winston Tutwiler hurries out to keep up with the passing parade. The revels of the present oppose the reveries of the past. The spinster calls the departed tourists *canaille*. Perhaps they are. But in this deeply elegiac play such judgements are peripheral. The vision at the heart of *Lord Byron's Love Letter* is the inevitable erosion of life by time.

The once-attractive woman now struggling for survival and unable to forget the lost love in her past reappears in *At Liberty*[3] and *Hello from Bertha*. The ironic title of the former is a phrase from the advertisement that the unemployed actress Gloria Bessie Green has placed in a trade paper. In her early thirties and suffering from tuberculosis, she loved a man who died after losing both his legs in a freight-train accident. These facts emerge as Gloria talks with her mother in their shabby room upon returning from a date with a stranger. Like *Portrait of a Madonna, Hello from Bertha* is the last scene of Williams's story of the faded belle. In this case the genteel lady has been replaced by the gross prostitute. 'Hello from Bertha – to Charlie – with all her love' is the only message that the paranoid Bertha, threatened with eviction from her room in the St Louis brothel to which she has withdrawn for the past two weeks, can bring herself to send to the man in Memphis she cannot forget. Like Richard Martin in *Portrait* and Shep Huntleigh in *Streetcar*, the fictional past admirers to whom the heroine appeals before her removal to an asylum, Charlie is less a real person than a dream of past happiness.

The title character of *The Lady of Larkspur Lotion*, although she partakes of the refinement of Gloria Bessie Green, is, like Bertha, a prostitute under threat of eviction. The Belle Reve of Mrs Hardwick-Moore, a dyed blonde of forty, is a Brazilian rubber plantation to whose quarterly revenues she insists that she is heir. But her down-to-earth landlady, Mrs Wire, is prepared to wait no longer for the rent on the wretched furnished room in New Orleans where the play is set. After a vagabond writer from the next room achieves a temporary rescue by forcing the landlady out, he too is revealed to be a pathetic creator of fantasies.

A Chekhovian blend of pathos and humour defines the tone of *The Lady of Larkspur Lotion*, especially in its last moments. The derelict lady and the derelict artist open a conversation in which belief is suspended, doubt and suspicion laid aside. Mutual acceptance at face value is its premise – he for a great writer, she for a great lady. They say to one another, as Blanche DuBois would put it, 'what ought to be the truth'. The form is comic and outlandish but the intention behind it is courteous. Among the flying cockroaches in the sleazy rooming-house from which they may both be evicted in the morning, the faded belle and the wanderer enact the ceremony of good manners, which derives from the sensitivity and consideration without which human life would be intolerable.

The homeless prostitute with dreams of past glory reappears as the eloquent and histrionic Willie in *This Property is Condemned*. In *Where I Live* Williams remembers a time he once saw a group of little girls on a sidewalk in Mississippi all dressed up in their mothers' and sisters' finery – old party frocks, fancy hats, and high-heeled slippers – mimicking a gathering of Southern ladies in a parlour. One little girl, not satisfied with the attention she was getting, stretched out her arms, threw back her head, and shrieked, 'Look at me, look at me, look at me!' before falling down from her heels in a heap of soiled white satin and torn pink net. He wonders if she grew up to become a Southern writer. Whether she did or not, there is no doubt that the little thirteen-year-old girl who appears in

47

the glad rags of her dead sister – blue velvet gown, dirty lace collar, silver kid slippers, dimestore jewellery – and tumbles down from the railroad track along which she has just made her precarious entrance is not only the main attraction but also the poet and story-teller of a play the names of whose only characters – Tom and Willie – virtually spell out the playwright's own.

Only telephone poles and leafless trees, a dilapidated house, and a sign reading 'GIN WITH JAKE' break the monotonous horizontals of the railroad track and the flat Mississippi terrain as, bit by bit, Willie unravels her story to the fourteen-year-old Tom, who serves as her audience. She is the sole survivor of a family of four. Her mother ran off with a railroad man, her father took to drink and disappeared, and her sister, whose memory she exalts, became a prostitute and died young. In the family house, which is now condemned, Willie continues to live as a scavenger. Once the story is told, she goes back along the track in the direction from which she came, and Tom is left alone to fly his kite.

There is not a trace of sentimentality in the dialogue. The lyric naturalism of the play comes from the candid conversation between the two children, a conversation whose repetitions and circularities – accompanied by the occasional sound of crows overhead or a locomotive in the distance – function like the recurring themes of a tone poem. The most frequent allusions are to the white sky and the blue heaven. Four times in the play Willie says the sky looks white as a clean piece of paper, and five times she sings a fragment of Alva's favourite song, 'You're the Only Star in my Blue Heaven'. Both allusions are to the purity of the sky above, day or night, in contrast to the cindery earth below from which the children regard it. Romantic aspiration lies behind the familiar theme of *belle rêve* and sordid reality. The song, which gains resonance from dramatic context, turns into a haunting piece of poetry. As a statement of exclusive love, it is an ironic choice for a prostitute; yet Alva is the only star in Willie's life. The little girl says her sister was beautiful as a movie star, and three times contrasts her death with that of Camille in the Garbo film. No music played, no flowers were sent, no loyal admirers stood by when the real prostitute, like the movie one, died of tuberculosis. Twice she says that Alva was 'the Main Attraction' at the house, an epithet from the lingo of show business that links the dead sister again to Garbo – a poor Southern Gothic version of Camille.

Other repetitions help to define the decadent world of *Property*. The railroad men who were Alva's customers, the brakeman with whom the mother ran away belong to the same landscape through which the Cannonball Express twice passes. Its lonely whistle in the distance suggests the unspoken grief that lies under Willie's excitement over her solitary games. Solitude is also the condition of the twice-mentioned schoolteacher, Miss Preston, who, Willie says, could not find a man to marry her. The women in the play are either lonely spinsters, hapless prostitutes, or disappointed wives.

Whether or not Willie herself is already a prostitute, she is clearly, like the property in which she illegally resides, condemned. Twice Tom asks her if she still lives in the house and twice Willie affirms that she does. The repeated exchange insists on the familiar theme of eviction and defines Willie as an outcast of the fugitive kind. It also points to the play's title, whose wording comes not only from real estate but also from show business. Agents speak of scripts and artists as 'properties'. Alva, the Main Attraction, had been for rent. Willie is doomed to follow her sister into a life of prostitution and, chances are, a short one.

Willie is really a kind of child Blanche DuBois. The cast-off finery in which she appears on the railroad track corresponds to what Stanley calls the 'worn-out Mardi Gras outfit' that Blanche wears in the Quarter on the night he rapes her – evening dress, silver slippers, rhinestone tiara. Like Blanche, Willie has already acquired a reputation for loose behaviour. Three times the name of Frank Waters comes up, a boy for whom she admits to having danced naked when she was lonely. Now she has inherited all of her sister's beaux, or says she has, and declares with pride that she will dance all night long at Moon Lake Casino and come home drunk in the morning. Three times she mentions the music in the house to which the railroad men thronged in the great days when Alva was alive. The once notorious place, now a condemned property, is in Willie's nostalgic recall like a lost Belle Reve.

This Property is Condemned was first published with *At Liberty* under the joint title of *Landscape with Figures*.[4] But, as in *Portrait of a Madonna*, the analogy with painting is ironic. The scene is indoors in *At Liberty*. The outdoor scene of *Property* is a long way from the restful vistas of traditional landscape art. The figures are not those of farm folk bending as they work the fertile earth, but rather those of children, one homeless, both truants, looking heavenward from a fallen world. Tom Williams's memorable picture of Tom and Willie is a vision of lost innocents in a wasteland.

Like the thirteen-year-old Willie, the eighty-five-year-old Aunt Rose of *The Unsatisfactory Supper* or *The Long Stay Cut Short* is a homeless outcast. The alternate titles of the sombre, elegiac play in which she appears define the archetypal actions of Williams's dramatic world: the eviction and the spoiled occasion. Having failed to please the relatives on whom she depends with either her cooking or her plans to decorate their house with flowers on Sunday, she is served notice by them that she must leave in the morning.

Aunt Rose, who looks like 'a delicate white-headed monkey', is one of Williams's aging spinsters, although not one of those with a lost love unless it is the unrequited love that she has given to her family throughout the long years of her past. She tries desperately to be of good cheer and good use to her begrudging niece and niece's husband, Baby Doll and Archie Lee Bowman, the big 'children' in whose home she has recently been cooking. Out of her struggle for survival emerge the familiar themes of present and past, life and death, *belle rêve* and ugly fact. She calls the roses she cuts from the bush 'my' roses and 'poems of nature', the stove on which she has put the greens for supper but which she has forgotten to light 'my' stove. The children are not interested in the roses and they are resentful of her delusions of ownership. The harsh truth is that she is homeless, enfeebled with age, and unwanted.

The little play's double action of spoiled occasion and eviction directly anticipates the birthday-party scene in *Streetcar*, in which Stanley gives Blanche the present of a one-way ticket back to where she came from. The blood relative in each case – a niece, a sister – sides with the husband but takes a softer line. The crude Archie Lee, like Stanley, puts matters brutally. His table manners provoke the criticism of his wife. He is jealous of his property, spiteful, and quick to anger. Indeed he warns Baby Doll that if the old woman dies in the house he will have her burned and her ashes put into an old Coca-Cola bottle. It would be difficult to find an uglier thought in Stanley Kowalski.

Although a good deal of the dialogue in *Unsatisfactory Supper* is comic (the lazy couple's gossip about their

51

relatives, Aunt Rose's recipe for Eggs Birmingham, the flap over Archie Lee's sucking his teeth), the non-verbal elements of the play conspire to project the prevailing mood of 'grotesque lyricism' appropriate to Williams's Southern Gothic elegy. Prokofiev-like music opens the scene and sounds occasionally throughout. A stage direction instructs the Bowmans to read their dialogue before the entrance of Aunt Rose 'like a grotesque choral incantation'. They later become 'the tribunal' on the front porch before which the old woman stands condemned to exile. Aunt Rose's singing the first two lines of the hymn 'Rock of ages, cleft for me / Let me hide myself in thee', defines her condition and points to her struggle. She says that when the time comes a wind will take her away like a faded rose. As the blue dusk turns to purple and then to black during the play's last moments, an unrealistic pool of light on the 'somehow sinister-looking' rose bush, which the approaching tornado will soon strip bare, states that the time is now at hand for the old woman, who stands in the yard Lear-like, shut out by her kin and exposed to the fury of the elements.

Williams's early one-act plays advance his dominant themes: soul and body, dream and reality, past and present. Their construction reveals his archetypal actions. Their use of light and music shows the influence of film. In the first group, the faded belle appears as lovelorn spinster, hapless prostitute, homeless aunt. In the second the wanderer appears as struggling artist, male sex object, guilty son. Within the more varied second group, however, one play is in verse, one focuses on a character based on Williams's father, and two others are experiments in comedy and romance to which Williams would later return in full-length plays that reverse his usual patterns.

2. Sketches of the Wanderer and Others

27 Wagons Full of Cotton belongs in the second group because, although the heroine (Flora Meighan) bears some resemblance to the faded belle, her humiliation takes a comic form. A retaliatory rape is at the centre of a vengeful Oedipal vision cast in the guise of a ribald tale. Flora is a plump, childish woman married to a 'large and purposeful' man of sixty (Jake Meighan) who runs a small cotton gin in the Mississippi Delta. He burns down the Syndicate gin because its competition threatens his livelihood. The next day the Syndicate superintendent (Silva Vicarro), who suspects Jake of arson, brings over twenty-seven wagons of cotton to be ginned and in a Boccaccian tit-for-tat has his way with the wife while the husband is working. The corpulent Flora has about as much ability to withstand the sadistic advances of the wiry, whip-brandishing little man as a big piece of cotton or the other things whose softness and whiteness suggest her maternal, infantile, and vulnerable quality – a lowing cow, a wad of tissues, a slice of angel-food cake, a white kid purse that substitutes for a doll. Like the heroines of the first group, Flora is a childless, unworldly, neurasthenic female. But, whereas they are poignant figures touched by farce, she is a farcical character touched by pathos. The raucous spirit of *27 Wagons* completely absorbed the elegiac mood of *Unsatisfactory Supper* when Williams combined the plots of the two one-act plays in his only original screenplay, *Baby Doll* (1956), which Elia Kazan directed. The heroine becomes an attractive ingenue (Carroll Baker) who prefers the playful but kindly Syndicate superintendent (Eli Wallach) to the oafish senex (Karl Malden) with whom she has yet to consummate her early marriage. The rape becomes an equivocal seduction. Aunt Rose (Mildred

Dunnock) is a supporting character who survives to cook another day in a film that celebrates the classic comic action of youth's triumph over age.

Whereas in *Baby Doll* the paternal figure is outwitted and displaced, in *The Last of my Solid Gold Watches* he is destroyed. First published in 1943, six years before the premiere of Miller's *Death of a Salesman* in New York, *The Last of my Solid Gold Watches* is exceptional among the early one-acters in having an old man carry the elegiac statement of the play. The massive figure of Mr Charlie, 'last of th' Delta drummers', derives from Williams's father. Like C. C., whose initials he shares, Charlie Colton is a travelling Mississippi shoe salesman of impressive size and power, who thrived during 'the great days of the road'. He had once moved with 'a tidal ease'. Now at seventy-eight, with perforated stomach and weak heart, he 'puffs and rumbles' toward his end in a changed world.

Nearly a half century of social and economic history has taken place since Mr Charlie started out in the last decade of the nineteenth century. He looks back nostalgically to a time when the 'All Leather slogan' sold shoes. Now all that matters is 'Style! Smartness! Appearance!' He has seen the principle of built-in obsolescence enter American manufacturing and mass production displace quality with quantity. The young salesman Harper, whom he fails to impress with these observations, is proof to Mr Charlie that the 'All Leather slogan' is obsolete among men as well as shoes. Strength of character no longer matters. He has lived through the First World War and the economic boom that followed, and he is bewildered by the Keynesian economic policy of the Roosevelt administration in dealing with the Depression.

Mr Charlie's significance as the representative of a bygone era gains resonance from his comparison to a fallen king. He recalls the days of the legendary past when he came in town 'like a conquering hero'. He held court amid the laughter and shouting while the liquor flowed freely during the all-night poker-games in his hotel room. It was 'a *throne-room*' then. The road was a royal road. He still moves with 'a kingly dignity of bearing'. But now his powers are waning, his days are numbered on the Delta, and Camelot has vanished from the territory that for so long had been his kingdom.

Mr Charlie's marvellous display of pocket watches, their chains festooned across his enormous paunch, exhibits his proud accomplishments during the golden age of his prime and simultaneously reminds him, like the now uncertain beat of his heart, that his time is running out. The signs of deterioration that surround him – torn blinds, broken fan, substandard merchandise – reinforce the theme of decline and fall. The deaths of contemporaries – customers, friends, fellow salesmen – show the beaten path to extinction. The quotation from Rimbaud under the play's title – 'Ce ne peut être que la fin du monde, en avançant' – states that the very end of the world is approaching. Mr Charlie, therefore, like the changes that have bewildered him, shows Williams's view of time as a process of decay and of life as a continual farewell.

The topical allusions to the federal agencies of the New Deal establish the decade of *Watches*. Several other early one-acters, set in the tenement rooms of industrial cities, also reflect the economic conditions of the middle thirties. *Moony's Kid Don't Cry* shows the restless spirit of the northwoodsman confined by the new responsibility of fatherhood. *The Strangest Kind of Romance* shows the allegorical Little Man as a lonely bachelor, unable to hold a job as a factory hand. (The play derives from the short story 'The Malediction'.) *The Dark Room* shows a troubled family of Italian immigrants as a social worker's case. The psychological statement of these Depression scenes transcends their message of social protest by presenting an ambivalent attitude toward the family: within it, freedom is stifled; outside it, one wanders alone.

This is the premise of *The Long Goodbye*, which was first produced in 1940 at the New School for Social Research, where Williams was enrolled. A year later he began work on 'Portrait of a Girl in Glass', the short story which formed the basis of *The Glass Menagerie*. The one-act clearly stands behind the full-length play in presenting a son's nostalgic memories of the mother and sister from whom he has been separated in the course of life. In this early treatment of the subject the son is the last to leave the tenement apartment in St Louis where he grew up. A series of flashbacks re-enacts the events which led to the dispersal of his family as Joe Basset, his suitcase packed to go, talks quietly with his friend Silva, a young fellow writer who stops by to offer him moral support, while upstage the burly, unsentimental movers take away piece by piece the furniture with which Joe has lived for twenty-three years.

The bed on which Joe and his sister, Myra, were born and their mother committed suicide to escape the ordeal of terminal cancer is carried out in dismantled sections followed by the big overstuffed chair in which their father sat in silence night after night listening to the radio before he suddenly abandoned them.[5] Bottles of perfume left on the dresser remind Joe of the attractive Myra, who moved north, where she now apparently lives on the favours of rich men, just as similar bottles in the store window of a distant city remind the wandering Tom of his sister's glass menagerie.

Children playing in the alley below and a radio next door tuned to a baseball game suggest the difference between the enchanted world of childhood to which Joe must say goodbye and the demanding world of adulthood in which he must struggle to survive. The movers, with their interest in the ball game, are a part of that rough male world, as is the boorish Bill, whom Myra met at a country club in Bellerive.[6] A child in the street calling, 'Fly, Sheepie, fly!' reminds Joe of the past when he and Myra played as children, and defines his role in the present as one of the fugitive kind. When there is nothing left in the flat but the ugly chandelier overhead and the torn and peeling wallpaper with its yellow stains exposed to the afternoon sun, a child in the street calls out 'Olly – olly – oxen-free!'

Like the child in the game, Joe has touched home base, but his freedom to emerge from hiding with the other players is equivocal. The homosexual flirtation between the hero and his friend (Silva says that Joe could pass for 'a female Imp' with a little hip motion) does not obscure the radical difference between them. Silva's attitude toward time is robust and practical. He welcomes the future as a chance to improve on the past. His WPA Writers Project assignments show that, like the Syndicate superintendent in *27 Wagons* whose name he shares, Silva plays to win by exploiting his opportunities. The nostalgic hero, on the other hand, cannot let go. Filial piety directs him to share with his sister the insurance money that his mother left specifically for him. He speaks vaguely of going to South America, but sentiment prevents him from selling the family furniture to help pay for the trip. The dispute between Joe and Silva defines the play's theme.

At the end Joe salutes the empty flat and goes out. He is about to become a reluctant wanderer through life and time, longing for what is gone, fearful of what is to come, never able to embrace the living moment. He may go as far as South America, but the memory of his past, like the old furniture in the warehouse, will remain stored in his heart at the cost of his freedom in the present.

The complementary plays *Auto-da-Fé* and *The Purification* also foreshadow *The Glass Menagerie*. The former presents a son's attachment to his mother, the latter a brother's attachment to his sister. Rosalio, the son in *The Purification*, may not be a writer, but he speaks of his incestuous love for his sister, Elena, 'in the language of vision' before committing suicide. Eloi Duvenet, the equally fanatical son in *Auto*, middle-aged and still living with his dominant mother, locks himself in and sets fire to the house when he discovers his latent homosexuality. Both plays derive their strong religious sense from Spanish Catholicism. *The Purification*, Williams's only play in verse, imitates Lorca. *Auto-da-Fé* (literally, 'act of faith') takes its title from the religious ceremony that accompanied the condemnation of the heretic by the Inquisition prior to his execution at the stake. The violence in the plays, however, is subordinate to their brooding elegiac mood. Behind the loss of childhood innocence an old order is cracking or already rotting away. In *The Purification*, the original settlers, Indian fighters, established an aristocracy that has now begun to intermarry with the labouring class that used to repair its fences. In *Auto-da-Fé* the property has lost all its value on the block in the Vieux Carré, where mother and son live in an old frame cottage of such sinister antiquity that even the plants and flowers along its low balustrade suggest a richness of decay. They speak in incantational tones about the corruption that surrounds them as juke-box music and shouts of laughter may be heard from the neighbouring bars and night clubs of Bourbon Street.

Among the plays of this group, it is really only in his two comic fantasies that Williams exults in the triumph of the living present over the dead past. The violets in the mountain have broken the rocks when Kilroy and Don Quixote march off together at the end of *Ten Blocks on the Camino Real*. The roots of the plum tree have broken the stones of the highway wall where Dorothy Simple agrees to meet her bold lover in *The Case of the Crushed Petunias*. Such exceptions only prove the rule that Williams's great theme is not growth but decay, not ascension but decline. The ironically titled *I Rise in Flame, Cried the Phoenix*, the playwright's tribute to D. H. Lawrence, focuses not upon the heroic life of the novelist but rather upon his bitter death.

Like modern short stories, the early one-act plays are lyrical revelations of character and situation written with the economy and precision their brevity requires. The dominant emotion is painful solitude. The typical action consists in the performance of a character before a less-than-enthusiastic audience. The performance is always the telling of the character's story, and its reception is always mixed or poor. Thus Charlie Colton's elegy for the old days gets a nod from the porter but leaves the shallow Harper unmoved. Lucretia Collins's tale of lost love touches the kindly Nick but only amuses the callous Frank. Bertha's exhibition of heartbreak and paranoia has the respectful attention of Lena but tries the patience of Goldie. Mrs Hardwicke-Moore's impersonation of a lady temporarily out of pocket is accepted by the Bohemian writer but rejected by the business-like Mrs Wire. Willie's grotesque miscasting as a happy-go-lucky prostitute does not quite convince the candid Tom. The recitation of Irénée de Poitevent's romance – in this case the character employs a surrogate – intrigues the foolish matron but fails to wake up her sleepy husband.

Seen in this light, *Love Letter, Property, Larkspur*

Lotion, Bertha, Madonna and *Watches* are plays within plays or at any rate performances within performances. Since the performance is never more than an equivocal success and most often a pathetic failure, the action illustrates a variety of the spoiled occasion. In *Long Goodbye* and *Unsatisfactory Supper* the idea persists of a negative response to a kind of theatrical effort. Aunt Rose's eagerness to make a production of everyday life antagonises the mean-spirited Archie Lee. Nor can the tough-minded Silva countenance Joe's 'Elegy for an Empty Flat', to whose enactment we are witness. The eviction or loss of home then combines with the spoiled occasion to complete the drama of defeat and alienation. Joe, Lucretia, Bertha, Aunt Rose and Mrs Hardwicke-Moore must all give up their domiciles; it is doubtful that Irénée and Ariadne can keep theirs for long; and the once regal Charlie Colton, banished by time from his kingdom, is a stranger in a strange land. Within the canon of Tennessee Williams the early one-act plays are essential and seminal works.

4
'The Glass Menagerie'
(1944)

TOM WINGFIELD. I didn't go to the moon, I went much further – for time is the longest distance between two places.

The first production of *The Glass Menagerie* opened in 1944 at the Civic Theatre in Chicago and in the following year at the Playhouse Theatre in New York. It was directed by Eddie Dowling and Margo Jones with Laurette Taylor as Amanda, Julie Haydon as Laura, Eddie Dowling as Tom and Anthony Ross as Jim. The music was by Paul Bowles and the set and lighting by Jo Mielziner. The 1948 London production was directed by John Gielgud with Helen Hayes as Amanda. The 1950 screen version was co-written by Williams and Peter Berneis, and directed by Irving Rapper with Gertrude Lawrence as Amanda, Jane Wyman as Laura, Arthur Kennedy as Tom and Kirk Douglas as Jim. In major revivals of *Menagerie*, Amanda has been played by Helen Hayes, Maureen Stapleton and Jessica Tandy. A television adaptation was produced in 1966 with

Shirley Booth, and another in 1973 with Katharine Hepburn.

In the play, a young merchant seaman (Tom Wingfield) looks back on his life before the outbreak of the Second World War. He had shared a small apartment in a poor section of St Louis with his sister (Laura), a painfully shy girl who spent most of the time polishing her glass collection, and his mother (Amanda), a minister's daughter from Mississippi whose husband, a telephone-company employee, had deserted her. Tom, who serves both as the narrator and as a participant in the enactment of his memories, was in those days a would-be poet working as a clerk in a warehouse to support the family. All that occurs in *Menagerie* is that the friend Tom brings home to meet Laura (Jim O'Connor), although he happens to be the boy she secretly admired in high school, turns out, unfortunately, to be already engaged.

The play is cradled in the playwright's recall of the Depression years when he worked in the warehouse of the International Shoe Company by day and wrote by night. The faded belle as doting mother derives from Miss Edwina. The absent father who fell in love with long distance alludes to C. C. during his happy days as a Delta drummer. Rose Williams's short-lived business studies, disappointing relationships and withdrawal from life inform the character of Laura as the predestined spinster with a lost love. Even the title refers to the collection of little glass animals that Rose and Tom kept in her room in St Louis, tiny figurines that came to represent for him all the softest emotions that belong to the remembrance of things past.

The theme of this gentle confessional work is aspiration and disappointment. The action is contained in the dashing of Laura's hope for romance, anticipated in the break-up of

Amanda's marriage, and echoed in the failure of Tom's effort to become a writer. The plot centres on Laura's non-Cinderella story. A shy, crippled girl encounters in the flesh the very man she loves, who leads her on and quickly lets her down. The exposition of Amanda's ideal girlhood in Blue Mountain and unfortunate middle age in St Louis is like an organ point that sounds the play's nostalgic note. She was once the belle of the ball, surrounded by suitors, and is now a deserted housewife, struggling for survival. As the disillusioned narrator, Tom looks back to a time when adventure and success seemed possible. Even Jim, although not discouraged, finds life after adolescence disappointing.

The historical setting provides an enveloping action that ironically reflects the play's theme. The economic recovery following the Great Depression came with the Second World War. The optimistic phrases in which Jim forecasts his future – '*Knowledge* – Zzzzp! *Money* – Zzzzp! – *Power*!' – hint at the sounds of battle. The customers of the Paradise Dance Hall across the alley from the Wingfield apartment house find an end to boredom in a hell on earth. Tom gets his wish to live the life of a hero in an adventure movie through his role as a merchant seaman in a world lit by lightning.

The full historical background extends from the Second World War, in which Tom serves, to the First World War, in which his father served before him, and even to the American Civil War, which ended in the fall of the Old South, to whose vestiges of gracious living his mother still so desperately clings. Amanda Wingfield is an anachronism in the St Louis of the 1930s and may even have been one in the Blue Mountain of her girlhood. Besides the story of her failed marriage, she brings to the play the sense of a world that, like herself, has long since faded. Her expectation that she would marry a wealthy planter and settle down to raise her family on a large plantation with many servants is a *belle rêve* of Southern aristocratic life in antebellum times. Her reminiscences are a confusion of wish and reality consistent with the play's premise that memory is primarily seated in the heart.

The Glass Menagerie is a dramatic elegy that plays within three concentric spheres of time: the time of the Second World War, in which Tom speaks to the audience as a merchant seaman; the time of the Depression, in which Tom lived with his mother and his sister in St Louis; and the time that Amanda thinks of as a vanished golden age – her girlhood in the rural South before the Great War. Like Tom's, the memory of her cherished past is partly enacted when she appears for the evening of the dinner party with a bunch of jonquils on her arm and skips coquettishly around the living-room, dressed in the girlish frock of yellowed voile with blue silk sash in which she led the cotillion long ago, won the cakewalk twice at Sunset Hill, and went to the Governor's Ball in Jackson.

The primary conditions of Amanda's poignant resurrection of her youth – spring and courtship – conform to the conventions of pastoral romance. Invitations poured in from all over the Delta that enchanted season when she had her craze for jonquils. In the evenings there were dances, and in the afternoons picnics and long carriage rides through the countryside, lacy with dogwood in May, and flooded with the jonquils that she made her young men help gather for her. On a single Sunday afternoon in Blue Mountain, she had seventeen gentleman callers, and extra chairs had to be brought in from the parish house to accommodate them. She could have become the wife of the brilliant Duncan J. Fitzhugh or of the dashing Bates Cutrere, who married another after Amanda refused him but carried her picture on him until he died. Amanda's arias on the lost dreams of her youth echo spring rites and tall tales of princesses wooed by many suitors.[1] Tom's memory of his mother's memory modulates easily into legend because it is twice removed from reality, recessed within the play's innermost sphere of time.

The Christian symbolism with which *Menagerie* is filled suggests that the time of Amanda's youth, the time of the Depression and the time of the Second World War are analogues, respectively, of Paradise, Purgatory and Hell. From the midst of global conflagration Tom looks back to the years of trial in St Louis that followed the disappearance of the Edenic South his mother remembers. The idea of the gentleman caller as saviour is clear from the 'Annunciation' to Amanda by her son that Jim is coming to dinner. One night at the movies Tom sees a stage magician turn water into wine and escape from a coffin. Amanda exhorts her children to 'rise and shine' and calls her ailing magazine-subscribers 'Christian martyrs'. In an atmosphere that is relatively dusky, the light on Laura has a pristine clarity reminiscent of that on saints in medieval paintings. The qualities of intimacy and reverence combine in her scene with Jim, the only light for which is provided by a candelabrum that once stood on the altar of a church.

As the gentleman caller does not fulfil his role as redeemer, the altar candles in Laura's heart are soon extinguished. The play's central image – light playing on a broken surface – suggests the ephemeral nature of life, beauty and human feeling. Joyful moments flicker only for an instant within the surrounding darkness of eternity, as when Jim and Laura look at the little glass unicorn together by candlelight, Amanda wishes on the moon, or couples find brief comfort in fleeting intimacy at the nearby dance hall, whose glass sphere, revolving slowly at the ceiling, filters the surrounding shadows with delicate rainbow colours. In the dim poetic interior of the Wingfield living-room, the picture of the absent father with smiling doughboy face is intermittently illuminated, while outside, beyond the dark alleyways and murky canyons of tangled clotheslines, garbage cans, and neighbouring fire escapes, the running lights of movie marquees blink and beckon in the distance. The movies themselves are no more than images of light that pass quickly into oblivion like cut jonquils or spring showers. For even art in *The Glass Menagerie* is presented as a feeble consolation for the sorry transience of life – fragile glass, scratchy phonograph records, scraps of poetry scribbled on shoe boxes.

Like the spotty, shadowy lighting, other extra-literary effects, drawn principally from film, emphasise the first condition of the play, which is nostalgia, and help to project the sense of an insubstantial world, wispy as memory itself. Transparent gauze scrims, one representing the outside wall of the tenement, another the portieres in the archway or second proscenium between the living-room and dining-room up stage, not only make scene transitions cinematic in their fluidity but also create a stage within a stage within a stage – a use of space which relates to the idea of containing time within time within time. After Tom's introductory speech, the grim wall of the building before which he has stood fades out as the Wingfield living-room fades in behind it. In turn, the portieres upstage dissolve and separate like a second curtain or inner veil of memory as soft lighting slowly reveals the family seated at the dining-table. The first scene is played without food or utensils. The last is played without words. During Tom's closing speech, Amanda appears to comfort Laura as if behind sound proof glass, her studied gestures reminiscent of the silent screen.

The Glass Menagerie

Music from three sources weaves through the scenes, bridging the spheres of time. On the on-stage Victrola Laura plays the music of her parents' youth, records her father left behind. The dance hall mixes the hot swing of the thirties with the slow tangos of the twenties and the tender waltzes of Amanda's girlhood. The music to which Jim and Laura dance, 'La Golondrina', is the same Mexican waltz that Alma Winemiller sings on Independence Day 1916 in *Summer and Smoke*. Most prominent is the recurring theme that comes out of nowhere and fades away again in accordance with film convention, like the images in a reverie. It is primarily Laura's *Leitmotiv* and suggests her fragile beauty as does the spun glass with which she is also identified. Williams's idea of barely audible circus music is consistent with his central image of light glimmering sporadically in the void. The immutable sorrow of life persists under the superficial gaiety of the passing moment. The distant calliope, with its associations of sad clowns, trapeze acts and performing animals, is an invitation occasionally to escape into a garish, itinerant world of make-believe. Human creativity is once more presented in the most pathetic terms. Indeed the circus animals are continuous with the figurines of Laura's menagerie, whose tiny size on stage correpsonds to the remoteness of the fairground.

In the course of this memory play, some forty projections of images, speeches or titles associate the graphic with the verbal in the sometimes whimsical manner of the mind when in the relatively free condition of sleep or reverie. Williams's explanation notwithstanding, the projections do not make structural points but instead spoof the sentiment of the scenes in which they appear. A pirate ship, a magazine cover, or the gentleman caller waving goodbye are pictures that undermine the pathos of the play like the farcical moments in Chekhov. Since the first production, directors have almost without exception cut the device as an expressionist intrusion upon an essentially naturalistic work. Perhaps they are right. Yet the projections are indebted less to the German theatre than to the silent screen. Such lines as 'Ah!' or 'Not Jim!' and such titles as 'The Annunciation', 'The Accent of a Coming Foot' or 'The Sky Falls' appear to derive, like so much else in *Menagerie*, from the playwright's frequent movie-going in childhood.

The call in Williams's production notes for 'a new, plastic theatre' to replace the outworn theatre of conventional realism is essentially a manifesto of the cinematic stage. The writer is to become more visual. He is to use lighting to suggest mood and assert relationships – such as the clear pool of light in which the fragile and unearthly Laura sits while Jim, Tom and Amanda are having supper upstage. He is to bring in music from out of the blue or flash images on a screen in order to give a plastic, mobile quality to plays that are relatively actionless. The lyric naturalism of the twentieth-century play of sensibility depends for its theatrical expression upon the writer's imaginative use of the methods and resources with which motion pictures have enriched theatrical art.

This explains why the American theatre became more of a director's medium, like film, in the time of Williams. When Elia Kazan founded the Actors Studio in 1947, three years after *Menagerie*, it was for the purpose of training actors to give film-size performances. His successor, Lee Strasberg, would later train them in the requisite docility. Actors were to become more compliant, more 'plastic', like the scenery and the lighting through which the all-powerful director would express his predetermined 'concept'. The neo-Stanislavskyan American Method repudiates 'projection consciousness' as leading to oversized mannerisms put out of date by the microphone and camera.

It is partly the convention of film, although chiefly that of the short story, from which the episodic structure of *Menagerie* derives. The play is an adaptation of a film script (*The Gentleman Caller*) based on a short story ('Portrait of a Girl in Glass'). The seven scenes mingle with allusive narrative speeches to convey a casual sense of order that accords with the nature of memory. In neither the story nor the play is the tiny plot the point. It is the revelation of characters locked in time. This explains why nothing much happens in *Menagerie*. Its lyrical, non-linear form is rooted in the gently exfoliative 'Portrait of a Girl in Glass'. It is also rooted in a particular character's point of view, a technique common enough in fiction but atypical of drama. Since that character happens to be an aspiring poet in both the story and the play, an inclination to lyricism is obligatory.

'Portrait' is essentially a character sketch of Laura, as its title from the static art of sculpture implies. Her brother, Tom, remembers her from the time they lived in St Louis with their mother and he worked in a warehouse. Their father had long ago deserted them. Laura was a frightened, reclusive girl who appeared to exist in a world of make-believe. While decorating the tree one Christmas, she picked up the star that went on top and asked Tom if stars really had five points. She spent most of the time listening to her father's old records, polishing her collection of glass figurines, and rereading Gene Stratton Porter's *Freckles*, with whose hero, a young one-armed lumberjack, she carried on an imaginary relationship. He would drop by her room for an occasional visit just as her brother habitually did. When she was twenty, she was unable to face the demands of secretarial school. When she turned twenty-three, her mother asked Tom to bring a friend home to dinner in order to meet her. He turned out to be a hearty and befreckled fellow employee (Jim Delaney), with whom Laura, much to her family's amazement, got along famously because she confused him in her mind with the hero of the much-read book. Unfortunately, he was already engaged. Not long after Jim's visit, Tom lost his job at the warehouse, left St Louis and took to wandering. He became independent and succeeded in forgetting his home, although from time to time he thinks of his sister.

The revelation that Jim is already engaged becomes more pathetic in the play because Williams makes the gentleman caller into Laura's real rather than her imaginary love. Her abnormality is less mental but more physical. Instead of the obsession to reread the same book, she has the more playable handicap of a slight limp. It is particularly effective when she and Jim dance together by candlelight (they are never alone in 'Portrait') and accidentally break the glass unicorn's horn – a piece of business, missing from the story, that uses the play's titular symbol and suggests, among other things, the sudden collapse of male ardour upon the removal of maidenly defence.

'Portrait' is a wistful memory, *Menagerie* a moving elegy. The play gains power from an intensification of theme and a strengthening of logic in the progression of events. The three years that pass in the story between the mother's discovery of her daughter's truancy and the appearance of the gentleman caller are reduced to three months in the play, long enough considering Amanda's determination to find Laura a husband if she is not to be a secretary. In the story, Tom's departure is peremptory because it is not preceded by a climactic quarrel with his mother. Jim Delaney makes no thematic contribution of his own because he is not a former high-school hero like Jim O'Connor. The mother is a minor character with neither reminiscences nor a name. Nor are the Wingfields specifically from the South.

The Glass Menagerie combines Williams's two archetypal actions. The climax of the outer play is the spoiled occasion, the climax of the inner play the eviction or loss of home. Laura does not sit at table with Jim. The gentleman caller, having declined his hostess's offer of lemonade, leaves early to meet his fiancée. After all the preparation, Amanda's party is ruined. Tom's curtain speech reminds us that everything has happened within his memory, and we may be sure that it will do so again and again. Whether the two belles, one faded, one never having bloomed, manage to keep their home after his departure we can only guess; but it is clear that the wanderer has none apart from them.

In the play's last moments, Tom's two roles, narrator and participant, coalesce. Dressed as a merchant seaman, the one who broke free to seek adventure stands before the audience and admits that he is a haunted fugitive. He calls out to Laura that he has tried but not been able to forget her. The many cities to which he has sailed seem to sweep about him like dead leaves torn loose from their branches. A strain of familiar music, a display of perfumes in a store window, or simply a fragment of transparent glass is enough to remind him of what he has lost. Upstage, behind the gauze scrim which marks the outside wall of the St Louis tenement that was once his home, the mother and sister he left behind enact a scene without words, like silent ghosts, visible only to the eye of memory. Still facing the audience, he tells Laura to blow out the candles which light the dim interior. She does so, he says goodbye, but on his exit the elusive, nostalgic music that has dipped in and out of the scenes from the beginning breaks off without resolution. Tom's climactic realisation that he will play out his 'memory play' for the rest of his days is like the 'epiphany' in a short story by Joyce. His confession throws all of the events that have preceded it into a different light; or, more precisely, it casts them into a greater elegiac darkness.

The problem of playing *The Glass Menagerie* arises from the fact that, whereas from a dramatic critic's point of view it is Tom's play, from an actor's it is Amanda's. The same distinction applies to Shakespeare's *Henry IV, Part One*, which is Hal's play although Falstaff appropriates it in performance. While students are invited to see the work as the education of the Prince, actors ask to read for the fat knight or the fiery rebel. Similarly, although *Menagerie* is really the chronicle of the Son, its production record shows that it has nearly always been construed as a starring-vehicle for the Mother.

Laurette Taylor's legendary performance established the tradition. The first Amanda was a plump little woman of sixty with a bright, eager face, her grey hair cut into girlish bangs. From all accounts, her characterisation was a composite of vague, fluttery gestures, sudden pauses, and unexpected shifts in pace or stress. Her delivery was quiet. A good deal of the time she gave the impression of mumbling. Bit by bit, her subtle revelations of hope, sorrow, despair, decision, longing, annoyance, snobbery, playfulness, coquetry, fatigue and resignation merged into a stage portrait of such fidelity to truth that reviewers were at a loss to define its method. Garland of the *New York Journal-American* called it 'Duse-like in the poignancy of its serio-comic detail', Gibbs of the *New Yorker* said one hardly knew what to write, and Young of the *New Republic* confessed that its depth and spontaneity defied analysis.[2]

On the other hand, Eddie Dowling as the first Tom did not altogether succeed. The actor–director was a short man of nearly fifty with a still boyish face. His characterisation was evidently congenial and subdued. He read his narrative speeches straightforwardly, putting the house at ease with his off-hand manner and personal charm. Most reviewers praised his performance much as they did Julie Haydon's ethereal Laura and Anthony Ross's workmanlike Jim. But his double role made others uncomfortable. It seemed too derivative of the narrator–participant in John Van Druten's *I Remember Mama*, then running on Broadway, or of the narrator in Thornton Wilder's *Our Town* before it. Krutch of the *Nation*, who disliked the cinematic effects created by Jo Mielziner's set and lighting, took even greater exception to what he called the 'pseudo-poetic verbiage' of the narrative speeches. Young, however, blamed Dowling rather than Williams. The narrations, he believed, only appeared to be a mistake on the playwright's part because the actor did not read them from character. If they had been delivered with the 'variety, impulse, and intensity' they needed, then the whole story would have been different.

It was thirty years before Young's thesis was put to the test. In 1956 the younger and more matter-of-fact Tom of James Daly appeared opposite the spirited Amanda of Helen Hayes (she played the role three times). In 1965 the gentle and disarmingly simple Tom of George Grizzard appeared opposite the earnest Amanda of Maureen Stapleton (she played it twice). But, according to Kerr of the *New York Herald-Tribune*, Daly's Tom made the narrations seem 'a trace heavy', and according to Watts of the *New York Post* Grizzard was less effective as the commentator than as the participant.[3] The narrations were largely cut from the 1950 screen adaptation, in which the caustic Tom of Arthur Kennedy appeared opposite the musical-comedy Amanda of Gertrude Lawrence. A flashback showed Amanda as a young girl dancing with her many admirers. A close-up showed her as a giddy mother peeping through the curtain to see how Jim and Laura were getting on. The obligatory Happy Ending came when the lame daughter, accompanied by the gentlemen caller, went out to the Paradise Dance Hall and met a man of her own.

In 1973 Thomas L. King published a valuable article arguing that *Menagerie* belongs to Tom, who tricks the audience into shouldering the pain he exorcises by creating his memory play.[4] In 1975 Rip Torn, cast opposite Maureen Stapleton's second Amanda, made the only all-out effort to read the narrations from character. The curtain speech was the key to his portrait. The result was a wild, brooding, quirky, homosexual Tom who flung his words at the house like accusations. Torn's performance did not receive a unanimous welcome; but neither was it damned with faint praise. Those who attacked it were inclined to do so without reserve; others were as absolute in their esteem. Barnes of the *New York Times* was reminded of a Greek tragic hero, Kalem of *Time* thought it 'just right', and Watt of the *New York Daily News* made the telling observation that Torn was at his best in 'the beautifully written narrative sections'.[5]

At the end of 1983 Jessica Tandy, the original Blanche DuBois, played Amanda in a New York revival directed by John Dexter. She was seventy-four. It was a reserved, grandmotherly Amanda who, together with Amanda Plummer's far-gone Laura and John Heard's fidgety Jim, was at odds with the postcard prettiness of the production. No filmy gauze or dusky light made unclear for long the big, elegant set of Ming Cho Lee. The Wingfield apartment was a store window at Christmas exploiting our nostalgia for the

1930s. The menagerie itself was set on matching tables down right and left. Attractive bookshelves marked the exit, upstage of the telephone table. Lamps hung from the suspended ceiling, beyond which, in the distance, the abstract forms of buildings were visible. Paul Bowles's original music was used selectively. One soft roll of thunder announced the rain. Bruce Davison's blond, clean-cut Tom, although he occasionally imitated Williams's drawl, read most of his lines with swift precision. The decorative look of the whole extended from his handsome sweaters to the pink and yellow light in which the stage was swathed, and above it to the proscenium arch, where, for the first time in a major production, some of Williams's legends (and others not his) were periodically illuminated in a graceful script. Like one of Laura's statues, *The Glass Menagerie* had been handled like a little treasure and remounted for commemorative display following the death of the author at the beginning of the year.

5
'A Streetcar Named Desire' (1947)

BLANCHE DUBOIS. They told me to take a street-car named Desire, and then transfer to one called Cemeteries and ride six blocks and get off at – Elysian Fields!

The first production of *A Streetcar Named Desire* opened in 1947 at the Barrymore Theatre in New York. It was directed by Elia Kazan with Jessica Tandy as Blanche, Marlon Brando as Stanley, Karl Malden as Mitch, and Kim Hunter as Stella. The scenery and lighting were by Jo Mielziner. During the long run Uta Hagen and Anthony Quinn replaced the original leads. The 1948 London production was directed by Laurence Olivier with Vivien Leigh and Bonar Colleano. The 1951 screen version was written by Williams, adapted by Oscar Saul, directed by Elia Kazan, and, with the exception of Vivien Leigh as Blanche, filmed with the principals from the first Broadway cast. A ballet based on the play with choreography by Valerie Bettis was first performed in 1952. In major revivals of *Streetcar*, Blanche has been played by Tallulah Bankhead, Faye Dunaway, Rosemary Harris, Lois Nettleton, Claire Bloom, Geraldine Page and Shirley Knight. A television adaptation was produced with Ann-Margret in 1983.

Streetcar derives its title from the terminal stop of a tramcar, since replaced by a bus, that once ran through the old French Quarter of New Orleans. The heroine takes it to get from the railroad station to her sister's place just before the curtain rises. The story that unfolds in the play, however, has its beginning thirty years earlier. At about the time of the First World War, two daughters, possibly three, were born into an old Southern family of Huguenot extraction (DuBois) and raised at Belle Reve, the ancestral mansion outside Laurel, Mississippi, in or near Two River County. The mansion had been the centre of a great plantation in antebellum days. But the indulgence of decadent habits on the part of the men of the family in succeeding generations had so reduced the estate that nothing was left during the sisters' adolescence except the house itself and some twenty acres of land.

At the age of sixteen the elder sister (Blanche) eloped with a young poet (Allan Grey) with whom she had fallen deeply in love. Shocked by the discovery of his homosexuality, she told him – on the dance floor of Moon Lake Casino – that he disgusted her. Minutes later he shot himself by the shore of the lake. It was far too late by the time the sexually innocent girl realised why the boy had been reaching out to her for help. After the suicide of her young husband, she began a long series of shallow affairs. Two years before the outbreak of the Second World War, her father died and her sister (Stella), five years her junior, left home, married, and settled in New Orleans. Blanche remained at the family mansion, where her mother died not long after her father, then the possible third sister (Margaret), and finally an old cousin (Jesse).

The deaths took place during the war years. More and more lonely, the young widow sought distraction in fleeting intimacies among the soldiers of a nearby army post. Soon, however, the medical and funeral bills became too much for the dwindling estate to sustain. At last even the old house was lost by foreclosure. She had been teaching high-school English in Laurel. She now moved to a shabby hotel in town, where her grief drove her to drink, hysteria and nymphomania. When the fact came to light that she was having relations with one of her students, she was dismissed by the school and evicted by the hotel.

At the opening of the play, the thirty-year-old Blanche, having lost her youth, her husband, her inheritance, her home, her employment and nearly all her family, arrives in New Orleans to stay with her sister because she has nowhere else to go. She is taken aback to find that Stella lives in a small, dingy apartment on a slum street in the old part of town, having married an uncouth automotive-parts salesman of Polish origin (Stanley Kowalski), whom she met when he was a soldier during the war. In an effort to make a new start, Blanche finds a possible husband from among her brother-in-law's friends (Harold Mitchell, called 'Mitch'). But Stanley comes between them. At the end, having been raped by the man of the house in which she sought refuge, her mind unhinges, and she is removed for an indeterminate future to a public asylum.

The dramatic action presents the final phase in the downfall of Blanche DuBois. The plot is framed by her arrival in the first scene and her departure in the eleventh. In performance the scenes are usually grouped into three acts in order to allow an intermission between scenes iv and v and another between scenes vi and vii. Thus Act I (i–iv) ends with Stella in Stanley's arms despite his having beaten her while drunk the night before. Act II (v–vi) ends with Blanche in Mitch's arms, hoping that she may have found salvation. Act III (vii–xi) ends with Blanche's removal to the asylum. A stage direction at the beginning of Act II (scene v) in the Acting Edition states that the scene is a balance point between the two halves of the play: Blanche's coming in the spring and her leaving in the autumn. But it is more that that. It undermines what would otherwise appear to be a hopeful development for Blanche in the following scene with Mitch. It contains the row between the upstairs neighbours (Steve and Eunice Hubbell) and the revealing flirtation between Blanche and the Young Collector for the daily newspaper (the *Evening Star*). The first episode suggests that the Kowalskis' quarrel need not be taken so seriously, and the second that Blanche's sexual notoriety had better be. As a whole, the scene implies that, when all is said and done, Stanley's sex life is wholesome and Blanche's is degenerate. When, at the end of the following scene, therefore, Blanche says that she has found God in Mitch's arms, the moment is doubly ironic. She would probably not be satisfied with Mitch as a husband for long. She also knows that Stanley is on to her and will warn his friend to stay away. It is a foregone conclusion that she will lose in the contest with Stanley for Mitch just as she has already lost in the contest with Stanley for Stella. In the third act her downfall is accelerated. The second act ends not with an actual rise in Blanche's fortune, only with the illusion of one.

As a socio-historical play, *Streetcar* is indebted to Chekhov's *Three Sisters*; as a psychological drama, to Strindberg's *Miss Julie*. Like Chekhov, Williams shows the decline of the gentry through the lives of its daughters. Like Strindberg, he combines class and sexual warfare. Of the two sisters who appear in *Streetcar*, the younger is a wife and the elder is a schoolteacher, as they are in Chekhov, the probable third having died ten years ago in what Blanche calls 'that dreadful way'. The sexual duel between the underling and the lady ends with the defeat of the latter in both *Streetcar* and *Miss Julie*. In the Williams, however, it is not the woman so much as the man whose desire is mixed with hostility. Whereas Strindberg's suave Jean aspires to the aristocracy, Williams's unrefined Stanley would like to destroy it. He takes the same sexual pleasure in degrading Blanche as he has already taken in pulling Stella down from the columns. Like Jean, who realises that he still has the soul of a servant when he turns his attention back to the Count's boots, the touchy Stanley bristles at the charge of being 'common'. But the odds are all in his favour. Strindberg was writing well before the First World War, Williams just after the Second. The ex-master-sergeant is a member of the dynamic working class in post-war industrial New Orleans. The jobless widow is a refugee from the collapsed ruling class of the old agrarian South.

Stanley's animal vigour, realism and solid connection to the living present seem at first to contrast favourably with Blanche's neurosis, delusion, and nostalgic relation to the dead past. Seen in this light, he is the defender of hearth and home against a hysterical intruder whose rather imperious attitude is defined in her opening scene with the neighbourly Eunice. She has always been waited upon by her younger sister. When she reveals her bigotry by calling Stanley a Polack, he tells her off in a jingoistic speech that New York audiences in 1947 applauded.

Another reason audiences favour Stanley, at least in the beginning, while readers favour Blanche, is that laughs depend more on performance than do tears, and Stanley has most of the laughs in the play – at Blanche's expense. The mere presence of the slouching, grinning Kowalski on

1. Tennessee Williams.

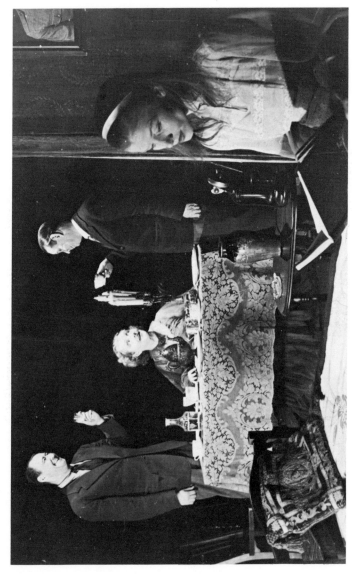

2. *The Glass Menagerie*, New York, 1945. Anthony Ross, Laurette Taylor, Eddie Dowling, Julie Haydon.

3. *A Streetcar Named Desire*, New York, 1947. Marlon Brando and Jessica Tandy.

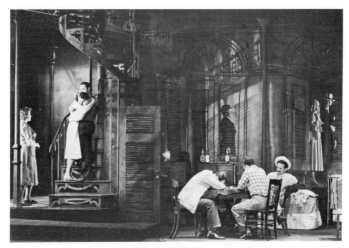

4. *A Streetcar Named Desire*, New York, 1947. Closing scene.

5. *A Streetcar Named Desire*, Warner Bros film, 1951. Vivien Leigh and Marlon Brando.

6. *Summer and Smoke*, New York, 1948. Margaret Phillips and Tod Andrews.

7. *Summer and Smoke*, New York, 1948. Alma (Margaret Phillips) bids farewell to Eternity.

8. *Cat on a Hot Tin Roof*, New York, 1955. Barbara Bel Geddes and Ben Gazzara.

9. *Cat on a Hot Tin Roof*, MGM film, 1958. Burl Ives and Paul Newman.

10. *A Streetcar Named Desire*, Warner Bros film, 1951. Vivien Leigh.

the same stage with his tense, fluttering sister-in-law is enough to arouse chuckles in the theatre. Throughout *Streetcar* comedy fulfils its classic purpose of reducing spirit to matter and violence to insignificance. The farce of the Hubbells' row, with its blows, chase and quick conclusion, is a comic inversion of the quarrel between the Kowalskis that leads to the physical abuse of the pregnant Stella on the poker night. The heavy-sweating Mitch, with his trips to the bathroom and boyish pride of height and weight, is a comic alternative to the courtly Southern gentleman. Blanche herself cadges a smile or two by mocking Stanley for his legalistic pretensions and noting that he was born under the sign of the goat. But in the comic duel between body and soul the triumph of the gaudy seed-bearer over the seemingly prim and proper lady is obligatory. When Blanche, in the middle of her shower, tells him to possess his soul in patience, he retorts that it is not his soul but his kidneys that he is worried about.

   In the course of the performance, however, the sympathy of the audience gradually shifts. Stanley's inadequacy as an egalitarian hero comes into focus in the final scene when he calls Pablo Gonzales a greaseball. His lecture to Stella on the regal command of the male in the home, an argument for which he cites the authority of Huey Long, would appear – at least in the light of Women's Liberation – nearly to outdo Blanche's own delusions of superiority. The premeditated cruelty with which he gives her a one-way ticket back to Laurel on her birthday comes from the same childish centre as his canine howling for Stella on the poker night. By the time he forces Blanche to bed while his wife is giving birth in the hospital, bestiality and cunning have all but obscured his appealing directness, good humour and physical well-being. In retrospect, neither his uxoriousness nor his protestation of friendship for Mitch rings true. Stanley's underlying motive for warding off Blanche's only suitor, we are bound to conclude, has been to remove the obstacle in the way of keeping the 'date' that he has had with her from the beginning.[1]

He is quite right in telling her that she accepted the date with him a long time ago. In their first scene together, Blanche regards Stanley's half-naked torso with awe as he changes his T-shirt in front of her. It is because she is torn between attraction and repulsion that she thinks she is going to be sick. The 'Varsouviana', echoing the guilt she bears for the suicide of her young husband, filters through the dialogue. The agent of her retribution and the prize of her rebellion against her genteel background coalesce in the figure of the swaggering Kowalski. Sex with her brother-in-law is the culminating event in a long period of sexual indulgence and self-degradation.

The brutal encounter of bodies is the opposite of the tender meeting of souls that defines the marriage of Blanche and Allan Grey. One reason Blanche's rebellion goes to extremes is that it was her sexual innocence, a result of her old-fashioned upbringing, that made her incapable of responding to Allan's half-spoken plea to be saved from homosexuality. She must punish herself for Allan's death; she must rebel against the repressive tradition that made her guilty of it; and, because she chooses to meet these demands by giving licence to her body, she must simultaneously punish herself for the betrayal of her soul.

The play renders in theatrical terms the divided self of its confessionalist author. The conflicting strains of puritan and cavalier in Williams's blood, which derive, respectively, from Miss Edwina and C. C., are dramatised in Blanche DuBois Grey and Stanley Kowalski. For that matter, Stella, who lives in a state of 'narcoticized tranquility' between the two with her chocolates, comic books and movie magazines, alludes to Rose Williams, who sank into an existence of semi-oblivious vegetation after her lobotomy. Obviously Williams invests himself in the hapless young poet whose sexuality is rejected by his inexperienced wife. It is for her failure to offer him what amounts to a maternal sanction that the otherwise devoted young Blanche, an allusion to the doting but strait-laced Miss Edwina, stands condemned. However, Williams's most famous faded belle, a woman endowed with both delicate beauty and literary taste, is primarily the playwright himself as a puritan renegade whose audacious promiscuity – in particular with younger men – bears the consequences of ostracism and humiliation in his early middle age.

Perhaps it is because *Streetcar* is exceptional among Williams's plays in not being the expansion of a one-act play or the adaptation of a short story that it has so firm a dramatic structure. The provisional title of an early draft, *The Poker Night*, remains the label for the third scene. Actually, there are two poker-games, one toward the beginning and the other at the end, working in counterpoint within the total design. In the first, while Blanche is winning Mitch, Stanley loses at cards, gets drunk, becomes violent and, finding himself isolated by the group, is thrown upon the clemency of his wife. In the second, Stanley wins at cards while Blanche, now psychotic, having lost both Mitch and Stella, and finding herself isolated by the group, is thrown upon the kindness of strangers.

The symbolic use of food and drink in *Streetcar* is further evidence of Williams's unusually careful dramatic planning. On the poker night, which marks the low point of Stanley's fortune in his contest with Blanche, the two sisters go to Galatoire's for dinner while the husband has a plate of cold cuts from the refrigerator. During the wretched birthday party, on the other hand, the husband feasts like a king while his wife has difficulty swallowing and his sister-in-law, having been presented with a ticket back to Laurel, runs to the bathroom, from which coughing and gagging sounds are heard.

The play begins with Stanley tossing Stella a package of meat on his way to the bowling-alley, a piece of business that establishes their sexual relationship by means of a bawdy joke. Minutes later, Blanche's addiction to alcohol establishes her secret shame. She has a stiff drink as soon as she is alone, at least two more when Stella returns, but declines a fourth with Stanley, remarking that she rarely indulges. The piercing scream that escapes from her when coke spills on her skirt before her date with Mitch is a striking illustration of her hysterical imbalance. The only direct indication of her sexual misbehaviour is her flirtation with the Young Collector, who, it amuses her to learn, escaped from the summer rain by stopping at a drugstore for a virginal 'cherry soda'.

Besides helping to define character, drinking, like the two card games, celebrates victory or registers defeat in the struggle between Blanche and Stanley. Stanley's reduction to a state of whimpering dependence in scene iii follows his drunken rage. Blanche's reduction to a state of helpless inertia in scene x follows her drunken histrionics. After Mitch leaves, having refused to take the symbolic Southern Comfort with her, Blanche dresses for the part of the main attraction at an imaginary drunken revel. Upon his return, Stanley opens a bottle of beer between his thighs so that the sudsy 'rain from heaven' gushes forth with phallic suggestiveness. Blanche declines his offer of a 'loving cup' and uses a broken bottle as a weapon in her last defence, thereby extending the prop's significance at the culmination of the sexual duel.

In *Streetcar* the eviction and the spoiled occasion – metaphors of man's essential solitude and of his painful disenchantment – are the events around which the play as a whole is built. The long story of Blanche's downfall may be seen as a process of dispossession that begins with her loss of Belle Reve, continues through the period of her abruptly terminated residence at the Flamingo, and, her way to a home of her own with Mitch having been blocked, concludes with her being forced off the premises consequent to the denial by her brother-in-law of further welcome in her sister's house.

The spoiled occasion provides the play's climax. The events of scenes vii–x all occur on Blanche's birthday. In scene vii, which immediately precedes the dismal party, Stanley tells Stella why Mitch will not be coming, while Blanche, ignorant of her impending disappointment, sings in the shower. Scene viii is the ruined festivity itself. An empty chair eloquently attests to the absence of Mitch. Blanche tries to keep up her end of table by telling a pathetic joke, during which the inattentive Stanley rudely continues to eat. Seconds later, after a rebuke from his wife for his manners, he hurls the dishes from his place to the floor. No scene in Williams better illustrates the playwright's characteristic action of brutal reality destroying feeble creativity. 'What poetry!' says Stanley when Blanche likens the blue candles on the cake to the eyes in the face of the son she hopes Stella will bear. On the brink of middle age, Blanche has made the effort to celebrate the day of her birth, to collect herself, to pause in life, and to dwell however briefly within the enchanted time that ritual sets off from the ordinary course of events. But the ritual cake is never cut nor are its candles ever fully lit, and the one birthday present she receives is tantamount to a summary notice of eviction.

The two contraries at the heart of the play – death and sex – coalesce in the scenes that follow. In scene ix Blanche confesses to Mitch that her husband's suicide led to her promiscuity. In scene x a single action marks the end of Blanche's life as a competent human being and the simultaneous gratification of her powerful attraction to Stanley evident from their first meeting. Indeed, the rape in *Streetcar* anticipates the violent wanderer plays – *Orpheus, Suddenly*, and *Sweet Bird* – by presenting the fulfilment of desire and the submission to a kind of death on a day of observance or festivity. The exultant Kowalski, having put on the red-silk pyjamas he saves for 'special occasions', forces upon his crazed sister-in-law an obscene celebration of his imminent paternity, for another birthday is about to be established overlapping her own. In the last scene a second Kowalski makes his first appearance on the stage and Blanche her final exit from it.

The ruined festivity in *Streetcar*, operating on the principle of blasphemous inversion, begins to suggest a kind of Black Mass. Other events, based on the idea of the spoiled occasion, are scattered throughout the play, creating a fallen world of lost hope in which imagination is futile and sensitivity fated to be crushed by mindless brutality. In scene iii the 'enchantment' that Mitch and Blanche create by putting a paper lantern over a naked light bulb and dancing to a Viennese waltz is aborted by the enraged Stanley. In scene vi Blanche and Mitch, having begun their evening in style and spirit (the Rosenkavalier presenting the traditional flowers), return from it in scene vii tired and disappointed (the shooting-arcade marksman carrying his plaster trophy). The final scene exploits the same idea. Half thinking that she is preparing to embark on a millionaire's yacht, Blanche dresses for the occasion in yellow and blue with a pin in the shape of a seahorse on her lapel. But her grateful leave-taking for a holiday at sea turns into her sad departure for a future in forced seclusion.

The exposure of the unprotected Blanche to cruel reality depends for its theatrical efficacy upon cinematic techniques that render the division between interior and exterior ambiguous. In Jo Mielziner's set for the original production, a gauze scrim on which windows were appliquéd formed the rear wall of the Kowalski apartment, a dingy, sparsely furnished two rooms separated by no more than a draw curtain hung below a broken fanlight. From the bedroom, left, a pair of steps led up to the bathroom off. From the combination kitchen and living-room, right, a low doorway gave upon a roofless porch above which a circular iron staircase, as if ascending to the Hubbells' apartment, disappeared behind the proscenium arch. Further right, an alley curved to the street that ran behind the house. There were over sixty light cues.[2] Dimming the area down stage of the scrim and illuminating the area above faded out the wall and faded in the street, Elysian Fields, with its pedestrian traffic of vendors, sailors and prostitutes. The mugging that foreshadows the rape was made visible by this means. The performance began with a montage in which Stella was discovered lounging in the bedroom and Eunice chatting with a neighbour on the stairs as a woman with a heavy shopping-bag crossed from down right along the alley to the street, where she could still be seen through the transparent wall, struggling under her burden, before making her way off up left.

Whereas in *Menagerie* passing through equivocal barriers had led to the nostalgic past, in *Streetcar* it exhibited the threatening present. Similarly, the music with which the heroine was associated expressed danger rather than seclusion. Laura's endless *Leitmotiv*, performed by a chamber ensemble, was reduced to Blanche's unfinished 'Varsouviana', played on a small electric organ. The polka and the waltz in *Streetcar*, both terminated by violence, seemed to point back to a more genteel epoch, or at least to the illusion of one, in a culture where even the occasional tunes from the neighbouring dance hall had been replaced by the relentless jazz from the bar and brothel.

The most spectacular feature of the original production was Marlon Brando's historic portrait of Stanley Kowalski, which not only became the hallmark of Method acting but also introduced a new type of hero to the national culture – the inarticulate, alienated, male sex object in work pants and T-shirt, whose line is rooted in O'Neill's *Hairy Ape* and extends through Ralph Meeker (in Inge's *Picnic*, notably with torn T-shirt), to Ben Gazzara, John Cassavetes, James Dean, Paul Newman, and beyond them down to countless imitations in and out of the Actors Studio. In the field of music the type is best represented by Elvis Presley, whose characteristic blend of hostility, unintelligibility and sexual exhibitionism achieves its final apotheosis in punk rock.

The first Stanley had the face of a poet, the body of a gladiator, and the vocal placement of a whining adolescent. Brando's performance was a mosaic of sexual insolence, sullen moodiness, puckish good humour and terrifying rage. His slurred delivery and loutish stances added to the grammar of acting. His deep concentration, like Laurette Taylor's before him, gave to his quick changes the appearance of constant fidelity to truth. Some were indelible. Audiences still remember the tiger-like suddenness with which Brando, in the birthday-party scene, having been told by Kim Hunter as Stella to help clear the table, smashed his plate, swept the dishes to the floor, stood up and, after an angry retort, stalked out onto the porch, all the while continuing to pick his teeth and lick his fingers. Nor have they forgotten his bellowing for Stella on the poker night after emerging from his cold shower onto the deserted stage, his T-shirt, torn in the preceding scuffle, clinging to one shoulder. His back was thereby exposed for the second time (the first being the opening scene with Blanche) as he knelt at the bottom of the circular staircase to await the slow descent of his forgiving wife. Hawkins of the *New York World-Telegram* remarked on the actor's 'astonishing authenticity'.[3] Brown of the *Saturday Review* called him 'all force and fire . . . a young Louis Wolheim with Luther Adler's explosiveness'.

As the first Blanche, Jessica Tandy was pale, thin, a little English, and never far from hysteria. Her stiff, slightly awkward gestures showed her fatigue and desperation from the time she arrived with her suitcase in the opening scene, dressed in a white suit with fluffy bodice, white gloves, handbag and hat, as if on her way to a garden party. Her wide-ranging voice seemed to vary almost as much in tone as it did in pitch, creating thereby the effect of constant breaking, or, in excitable moments, even of sobbing. Barnes of the *New York Herald-Tribune* remarked on her 'haunting and volatile quality'. Coleman of the *New York Daily Mirror* called her portrayal a *tour de force*. Atkinson of the *New York Times* wrote that she played with an insight equal to Williams's own. The playwright, he observed, had taken no sides. He had created all his characters right in their way. Appropriately, therefore, the first Blanche made no clear distinction between sanity and reason, gentility and pretence. She caught on the wing 'the terror, the bogus refinement, the intellectual alertness and the madness' that could 'hardly be distinguished from logic and fastidiousness'.

It was precisely for not making those distinctions that she

was criticised by Harold Clurman. Williams's heroine, he wrote, was a poet and an aristocrat by virtue of 'the subtlety and depth of her feeling' and 'the sheer intensity and realization of her experience'. In contrast, her antagonist was simply 'the embodiment of animal force', oblivious to or scornful of anything beyond his scope. The trouble with the performance was that Jessica Tandy's appeals on behalf of human cultivation did not altogether sound genuine. At the same time, Marlon Brando's 'acute sensitivity' made his character too sympathetic. Because the Blanche was 'fragile without being touching' and the Stanley was 'touching without being irredeemably coarse', the audience sided with the antagonist until very nearly the end. Eric Bentley's response was similar. Brando was 'quite wrong for the part'. The playwright had created a brute, but the actor had given us 'an Odets character' whose tough talk was but 'the mask of a suffering soul'. The replacements, the illiterate and less humorous Stanley of Anthony Quinn and the more persuasively Southern Blanche of Uta Hagen, were in Bentley's view an improvement in casting.

Clurman's and Bentley's objections point to the central problem of playing *Streetcar*: what balance to strike between Blanche and Stanley for the allegiance of the house. If Blanche is portrayed as a neurotic and pretentious woman of whom history is well rid, and Stanley as a healthy animal whose brutishness is but a symptom of his 'acute sensitivity', then *Streetcar* becomes a melodrama, a work of social protest, or, as Bentley put it, a Group Theatre play. On the other hand, if Blanche is played as a distraught but gentle soul from a world of lost refinement, and Stanley no more than a brute, then the work is turned into melodrama of another kind.

Elia Kazan's dynamic production did not compromise

with Williams's rich portraiture for the sake of thematic clarity. Indeed, the director recorded in his rehearsal notes that it was essential for the heroine to be seen as 'the heavy' in the beginning.[4] We observed her bossiness and dependency, saw her bad effect on Stella, and wanted Stanley to put her down. Only later, when we came to understand her pain, to feel her desperation, and to appreciate her sensitivity and intelligence did we begin to realise that we were witness to 'the death of something extraordinary'. In Kazan's view, furthermore, the brutality of the crude brother-in-law sprang from self-hatred. He was 'deeply dissatisfied, deeply hopeless, deeply cynical'. To escape his silent frustration, he had built a hedonist life that he would defend to the death. He was bombarding his consciousness with sex, food, drink and sport. It was vital for Marlon Brando to make the props come to life: to take pleasure in opening a beer, finishing a meal or even changing a T-shirt. When Stanley's hedonism failed him, however, his tactic was to cut down anyone who pretended to be better. Ultimately, that is why he raped Blanche.

The 1951 screen version was hampered by censorship. Since the real problem with Allan Grey was a forbidden subject, a vaguely intimated weakness substituted for his homosexuality, making spurious his bride's sudden disgust with him. Since the rapist could not go unpunished, the film ended as Stella, her baby in her arms, ran up the spiral staircase never to return, and Stanley's futile protests below were soon lost in the closing music. On the other hand, the production gained from the delicate beauty and waif-like poignancy of Vivien Leigh, whose appearance as Blanche DuBois made iconographically consistent a new figure of American myth. The belle of Tara had become the outcast of Belle Reve.

As a matter of fact, *Gone with the Wind* was giving

continuous performances at popular prices on the Loew's circuit in New York when Irene Mayer Selznick, daughter of Louis B. Mayer and former wife of David O. Selznick, presented *Streetcar* in December of 1947. When the film version was released, Williams's play, like Margaret Mitchell's novel, entered the American consciousness. Vivien Leigh's Blanche DuBois, following her Scarlett O'Hara, showed the Southern belle approaching middle age in a refurbished version of the myth of the Old South's fall. As if magically and symbolically having lived through the three quarters of a century since Reconstruction, she reappeared as a disenfranchised gentlewoman from the aristocratic and pastoral South to suffer her final degradation under the occupation of the progressive and industrial North. In the film only the heroine herself and the Young Collector for the *Evening Star* sounded native to Louisiana or Mississippi. The New Orleans factory where Stanley and Mitch were employed clearly favoured hiring New Yorkers.

Social change seen as a process of deterioration is an elegiac view of history. The Grim Reaper, having made camp on the steps of the ancestral mansion, triumphs over the entire house of DuBois once the last of the line is removed to oblivion. Even before then, Blanche admits that Stanley may be the sort of man with whom she and Stella should mix their blood now that they no longer have the estate to protect them. Yet the play is less a lament for the world to which Blanche was born than it is a lament for the dream of it. The myth of the Old South that hovers over *Streetcar* is an intimation of paradise, a dim memory of sheltered ease, a *rêve* of youth and beauty that have waned with the passing years. An adolescent girl's shattered dreams permeate the atmosphere of lyricism and decay amid the faded elegance of the French Quarter, fragments of a childlike aspiration to a chaste and timeless love, like that of the two innocents who walked in the eternal spring of Eden with neither the fear of mortality nor the shame of desire. It is little wonder that the fabled mansion of Blanche DuBois, made of such stuff as fond dreams are made on, was lost to the realities – both 'epic' in measure – of death and fornication.

The belle whose radiant beauty in her youth turns into the faded looks of her age is Williams's central image for the sad transience of human life. The evening star, as Blanche learns, takes up collections, for at thirty the belle is no longer in the morning of her years and all followers of Venus must pay. The coin, appropriately, is passionate yearning, the inevitable frustration of desire by declining appeal. When Blanche tells the Young Collector that on a rainy afternoon in New Orleans, an hour is a piece of eternity in your hands, the focus shifts from a unit of local duration to a measure of potential experience. The fact that, in either case, it slips through the heroine's fingers reaffirms the play's elegiac theme. The fading belle is a victim of time longing for a future that will not be and for a past that never really was.

6
'Summer and Smoke'
(1947)

JOHN. What is eternity?

ALMA [*in a hushed wondering voice*]. It's something
that goes on and on when life and death and time
and everything else is all through with.

JOHN. There's no such thing.

ALMA. There is. It's what people's souls live in when
they have left their bodies. My name is Alma and
Alma is Spanish for soul.   (Prologue)

Both *Summer and Smoke* and *A Streetcar Named Desire*
were begun in 1945 and both were first performed in 1947.
However, the former received its world premiere in Dallas
and did not open in New York until the following year. The
Dallas production was directed by Margo Jones on the
arena stage of the Gulf Oil Playhouse with Tod Andrews as
John and Katherine Balfour as Alma. The 1948 New York
production was redirected by Margo Jones on the
proscenium stage of the Music Box Theatre with Tod
Andrews as John and Margaret Phillips as Alma. The

94

music was by Paul Bowles and the set and lighting by Jo Mielziner. The 1951 London production was directed by Peter Glenville with William Sylvester and Margaret Johnston. The 1952 off-Broadway revival was directed by José Quintero with Lee Richardson and Geraldine Page. The 1961 screen version was written by James Poe and Meade Roberts, and directed by Peter Glenville with Laurence Harvey and Geraldine Page. An opera based on the play with music by Lee Hoiby and libretto by Lanford Wilson was produced in 1971.

Summer and Smoke presents the second of Williams's three portraits of Alma. The first appears in 'The Yellow Bird', a short story published just before the Dallas premiere of 1947, and the third in *The Eccentricities of a Nightingale*, a substantial revision of the play written for the London premiere of 1951 but not performed until 1964. 'The Yellow Bird' is a comic fantasy about a minister's daughter (Alma Tutwiler) who kicks over the traces of her puritan upbringing and after a profligate life in New Orleans dies wealthy and happy. At the age of about thirty she peremptorily defies her father by taking first to cigarettes, then to cosmetics, then to alcohol, and finally to prostitution. She grows rich when her infant son (named John after her favourite lover) crawls out of her shabby room in the French Quarter and returns later with treasures of gold and jewellery from the sea. He grows up to be a sailor. When the time comes for Alma to die, her long-dead lover returns with a cornucopia of additional treasure and leads her away. At the Home for Reckless Spenders, to which she has bequeathed her fortune, a monument is erected composed of three androgynous figures astride a leaping dolphin named Bobo. One bears a cross, the second a lyre and the third a cornucopia. The name on the 'arrogant' dolphin's flank is that of the titular bird alleged to have been the devil's emissary by an ancestor of Alma's puritan father (one in a long line of ministers) as evidence against his wife in the Salem witch trial that condemned her. The image of Art, Religion and Plenty riding the irrepressible animal spirit is both an exclamation point at the end of Alma's success story and an exuberant affirmation of the cavalier cause for which she rebelled.

'The Yellow Bird' gives to *Summer and Smoke* its premise and its penchant for symbols. The play, however, is concerned less with allegory than with heartbreak. The heroine is not the self-assured rebel of the story but a neurasthenic Southern gentlewoman endowed with a delicate spirituality and an extraordinary tenderness, who tries and fails to win the man she loves. Williams keeps the first name, Alma (and that of the man in question, John), but because of its comic overtones he exchanges the surname for that of the condemned and mutilated Oliver Winemiller, hero of 'One Arm'. The drama unfolds in a multiplicity of short episodes which are enacted to intermittent musical accompaniment on a unit set that represents the town of Glorious Hill, Mississippi, under the changing skies of night and day. Clouds drift, constellations appear, and in the first scene fireworks splash (it is 4 July) on the overarching cyclorama. At opposite sides of the stage, the mere fragments of scenery indicating the rectory (right) and doctor's office (left) render ambiguous the distinction between interior and exterior. On the elevation at centre, within a park or square, the crouching figure of an angel with lifted wings (Eternity) is always visible, water flowing through its cupped hands to make a public drinking-fountain.

The cinematic stagecraft of *Summer and Smoke* accords with its discursive form. Indeed the work is possibly the best example in the canon of what Williams called 'the play of sensibility', a dramatic genre typified by 'the sensitive surface' and 'quiet progression' of fiction. The plot material of a novel, spread over a period of six months, may be glimpsed behind the twelve scenes. The Prologue alludes to a time fifteen years earlier. We learn that toward the end of the nineteenth century a son was born to the town doctor and a daughter to the Episcopal minister. From an early age the girl in the rectory loved the boy across the way, who responded by teasing or scorning her. The boy grew up without the mollifying influence of a woman, because his mother died of illness when he was very young. The girl assumed the duties of a minister's wife while still in her teens, because her mother suffered a breakdown that left her incompetent. The boy, John Buchanan, Jr, became a doctor like his father. The girl, Alma Winemiller, became an amateur pianist and singer known as 'the Nightingale of the Delta'.

In the summer of 1916 John and Alma have a brief encounter that comes to naught partly because the minister's daughter is struggling to come to terms with her repressed sexuality, partly because the doctor's son is going through a period of youthful self-indulgence, but chiefly because her consuming love for him is never requited. He is bored by the artistic and intellectual interests of her circle. She regards his drinking, gambling and lechery as 'a desecration'. John's behaviour changes abruptly when his father (John Buchanan, Sr) is shot by the owner of Moon Lake Casino (Papa Gonzales), whose daughter (Rosa) John was on the verge of marrying to clear his debts. The reformed John takes up his father's good work and becomes the town hero. The stricken Alma, whom John partly blames for the shooting because she had told the elder Buchanan what was going on, gives up her music and becomes a recluse. Early in winter Alma goes to John, confesses her love, and offers herself to him on any terms. He declines, already having become engaged to one of Alma's former pupils (Nellie Ewell). That evening in the park Alma strikes up an acquaintance with a young travelling salesman (Archie Kramer) and exits with him for a night at Moon Lake.

As an allegorical drama, *Summer and Smoke* presents the conflict of body and soul. John's father administers to the body, Alma's to the soul. Since John is a bacteriologist and Alma a musician, the soul is associated not only with religion but also with art, to say nothing of illness, eccentricity and superficial refinement. For its part, the body is associated not only with medical practice but also with science, to say nothing of health, normality and violence. The prissy culture-mongering of the club over which Alma officiates contrasts with the brawls and cockfights at the casino John frequents on Moon Lake.

But John and Alma are both in transition. Indeed, when he refuses her, at the end, he says that he has discovered the primary importance of the soul, or something like it, whose existence he had formerly denied. Yet, if 'the tables have turned', as Alma sadly replies, they have by no means done so evenly. She now wants his body, but he does not want her soul. It is true that he no longer pursues her. But then he never did, or, if he did, not for the reason he once thought. When pressed to explain just what the reason was, he can only grope for an answer. It was something, he says, that she could not have named and he could not have recognised, and even now he does not understand. In any case, he prefers the younger and more aggressive Nellie Ewell to the soulful fading belle, whose eyes and voice, he insists, represent the utmost beauty he has known.

Therefore, whereas Alma's change is fundamental,

John's is merely developmental. He pulls himself together after sowing his wild oats. She falls apart after losing the love of her life. The minister's daughter now pursues a nightly quest for sex with strangers, but, like Lucretia, Irénée, Bessie or Blanche, she will never get over her loss. Since childhood Alma has been in love with John, and since childhood he has derided and rejected her. The doctor's son combines the functions of Allan Grey and Stanley Kowalski in being both the object of the belle's soul's desire and the vigorously physical man who provides her punishment. The alliterative title, suggestive of heat on heat, toys with the play's allegorical underpinning and points to its elegiac action. Smoke alludes both to the fire of sexual passion and to the intangibility of the incorporeal soul. The passing from summer to winter (it is spring to autumn in *Streetcar*) affords a suitable accompaniment to the passing of Alma Winemiller from the brief bloom to the long decay of her chance for love.

The emphasis is not upon allegory but upon sensibility. Williams's strength is not the rigorous examination of ideas but the compassionate presentation of the painful moment. By showing a sensitive creature in a condition of loss and bewilderment, he achieves a pathos, often leavened with humour, that is reminiscent of Chekhov. In *Summer and Smoke* that condition is the heartbreak of Alma. If we step back from the play as an order of words and regard it instead as a series of images, what we see is a darkening world in which John is continually leaving Alma or sending her away. In the Prologue, when they appear as children by the fountain at dusk, he kisses her roughly, jerks her hair ribbon, and runs off with a mocking laugh. In scene i, when they reappear as adults in the same place, he teases her a bit, vaguely asks her out, and, the afternoon having turned into evening and the evening into night, leaves her to follow

Rosa Gonzales. There are no dawn scenes. In scene iii he breaks away from her club meeting. In scene vi, their one night out, he runs for a cab to send her home alone. In the climactic scene xi, having admitted she has always loved him, she goes from his office with the knowledge she has lost him for ever. The afternoon light is already fading. An hour later by the fountain, after picking up the salesman, she raises her hand first to the angel and then to the house in a valedictory salute. The real action of *Summer and Smoke* is not the conflict of body and soul but a continual farewell, or, as Williams would say, 'a Long Goodbye', framed in elegiac dusk.

Although they disagreed about the play itself, nearly all the reviews praised its original production on Broadway in 1948.[1] Atkinson of the *New York Times* described Jo Mielziner's scenery as 'a glorious setting of lightly penciled lines and curves as airy as the writing'. Krutch of the *Nation* wrote, the 'single, semi-representational set, dominated by a vast, star-studded sky, is not only one of the most beautiful but also one of the most usable multiple arrangements I have ever seen'. Clurman of the *New Republic*, however, thought that a realistic set would have been less confining to the imagination. He also criticised Margo Jones for not using her good actors well. The central characters came off simply as a 'cold' girl and a 'passionate' boy. As John, Tod Andrews, although handsome and earnest, had no real characterisation. As Alma, Margaret Phillips emphasised outward mannerisms at the expense of establishing main motivations. The *New Republic*'s reviewer was a minority of one. Atkinson wrote that the acting was deliberately 'light in style and appreciative in moods that appeared to be orchestrated'. The two principles created 'immense sympathy and wonder, binding the fragments of the play into a single strand of sombre, tragic emotion'. Margaret Phillips, by showing the essential nobility behind the appearance of desperation and silliness, had presented the stage with 'a masterpiece'. Krutch agreed that the production was brilliantly acted and directed. *Time* magazine called it a personal triumph for the twenty-four-year-old actress from Wales, noting the resemblance to Jessica Tandy in her slim body and strong, angular features.

The 1952 revival in Greenwich Village brought fame to a new association of Williams interpreters headed by the director José Quintero and the actress Geraldine Page, whose exquisite performance as Alma established her reputation as a leading exponent of the faded belle. She would repeat the role in the film and play the heroines in the first productions of *Sweet Bird of Youth* and *Clothes for a Summer Hotel*. The arena stage of the Circle in the Square, once the dance floor of an old night club, was ideally suited to Williams's cinematic conception. The fountain statue of Eternity seemed to have been hewn from the structural pillar at the centre of the main playing-area. The barely indicated settings around it made the many scene changes easy as dissolves. Overhead the cyclorama covered the town with changing skies. In the background, the primitive, raggy, early New Orleans jazz of Kid Rena helped to set mood and period. Off-Broadway had come of age.

In one way or another, all the reviewers of *Summer and Smoke* remarked on its affiliation with *Streetcar*. Krutch observed that the heroine was again 'an unhappy woman, passionate by nature but loyal in her conscious mind to the ideals of an anemic gentility'. Brown of the *Saturday Review* thought that Alma often suggested 'a first pale sketch of the woman who, after she had turned prostitute, became Blanche DuBois'. Coleman began his review in the

New York Daily Mirror by making the point unmistakable: 'If you want to know how the unfortunate teacher in *A Streetcar Named Desire* got that way, you should see Tennessee Williams's new and prefatory play.'

The fact is that *Summer and Smoke* and *Streetcar* form a diptych whose subject is the fading belle. The first shows her background, the second her downfall. In one she appears as a native resident of the small Mississippi town of Glorious Hill before the First World War, in the other a fugitive in the city of New Orleans after the Second. The dividing-line between the restraint of her early period and the promiscuity of her late is the loss of her first and only love. The last scene of *Summer and Smoke* shows Alma Winemiller newly dependent on the kindness of strangers. Where she leaves off, Blanche DuBois begins.

Alma, like Blanche, is an anachronistic character deprived of her youth. Difficulties at home require the belle in both plays to assume the responsibilities of the previous generation and result in her being out of step with the times. Blanche, having remained at Belle Reve in the effort to hold it together after the deaths of her parents, strikes us as a visitor from a world gone by when she comes to her sister's. Similarly, Alma, having filled in as hostess and homemaker for her regressed mother, seems quaint and prematurely spinsterish. She contributes her remarks on set topics such as the weather with the grace of one who prizes courtesy above 'the new integrity'. That she is mocked for her decorum indicates the awkwardness of her position as a lady in a world where the term itself already sounds dated. She is a teacher of music (Blanche is a teacher of English), an occupation that is consistent with her role as a custodian of culture against the onslaught of change.

The purely theatrical elements of the diptych help to

project the belle's background in *Summer and Smoke* as opposed to her later downfall in *Streetcar*. The thirty-year-old Blanche's desperate efforts to remain attractive are evident in the gaudy assortment of silks, jewellery and summer furs that Stanley discovers in her trunk and the crumpled evening-gown and rhinestone tiara in which she decks herself on the night he rapes her. Alma makes a modest step in the direction of allurement when she appears for her final scene with John (and for that matter her scene with the travelling salesman) in a russet dress and plumed hat, representing the beginning of her cavalier rebellion against the puritan heritage in which she was raised.

The conflict between the belle's traditional propriety and her natural desire results in the mild hysteria of her early period and the serious imbalance of her late. Whereas Blanche drinks, Alma relies on pills and handkerchiefs. Indeed her constant handkerchief – delicate, fluttery, ladylike – is both an essential part of her costume and a theatrical metaphor of her spirit. Handkerchiefs are also the tokens of love and rejection through which her story is told. John's refusal of Alma is the event of both their first and last encounter. At the start he scorns her childhood gift of a box of handkerchiefs. At the end his fiancée gives her a lace handkerchief for Christmas. Oblivious to its irony, Nellie selects a gift for her old singing-teacher that serves as John's pre-emptive denial of Alma's final plea.

The world of *Summer and Smoke* is spacious, that of *Streetcar* confined, indicative of the belle's relative mobility and power of choice in her early period opposed to her late. The multiple locations under the skies of Glorious Hill are a contrast to the cramped Kowalski apartment. The single location in *Streetcar* suggests the entrapment in life to which Blanche refers. Nor in fact is there a way out of the trap unless it is into a still narrower one. Special effects make visible her psychotic fantasies as if the room's very walls were threatening to close in on her. On the other hand, the special effects in *Summer and Smoke* – fireworks and stars – seem to expand an already ample space, and the statue of the Angel of Eternity, illuminated in the darkness between scenes, to imply an extratemporal perspective.

The greater variety of music adds to the sense of a milieu in which choice is still possible. At Elysian Fields there is little to challenge the dominance of the jazz from the Four Deuces. But at Glorious Hill the hymns and sentimental favourites Alma sings are not submerged in the flamenco and blues John prefers. Moreover, neither the songs of the plaintive spirit nor those of the restless flesh can subdue the martial airs of triumph and commemoration.

Indeed Christmas and Independence Day are the twin pillars of *Summer and Smoke*, providing an extensive ironic framework for the sufferings of the prematurely faded belle. Just as Blanche's private day of celebration is spoiled, the great public festivals of winter and summer are ruined for Alma. In July, during a night of band music and fireworks, John mocks her and leaves her for Rosa Gonzales. In December he rejects her for the daughter of the town's 'merry widow', home from school, and bubbling over with glad tidings of the season.

The nostalgia for a bygone age that underlies Williams's elegy for lost love and lost youth has its roots in his earliest memories. The move of the Williams family to St Louis in 1918 ended Tom's sheltered life in the rectories of the Reverend Walter Dakin and began his exposure to stern experience. *Summer and Smoke* takes place in the period just before the global conflict that, so to speak, ended the nineteenth century and launched the twentieth. The waning of what he construes to be the simpler and gentler world in which his parents were young, therefore, reflects the playwright's farewell to Edenic childhood. The theme of past and present overlays that of soul and body in the contrast between the minister's daughter and the doctor's son. Science in its ongoing quest for knowledge is progressive, religion in its emphasis upon lasting verities conservative. Alma Winemiller is a nineteenth-century woman with what Williams calls an eighteenth-century elegance. John Buchanan is a twentieth-century man. We do not, however, applaud his gain, but rather mourn her loss.

Water flows continuously through the cupped hands of the stone angel in *Summer and Smoke*, like the piece of eternity that slips through Blanche's fingers one afternoon in *Streetcar*. The winged, crouching figure, ostensibly benign, seems slowly to become more impassive as it broods, motionless, over the thirteen episodes of the play. The innocent young Alma is struck with wonder at its name, the heartbroken woman sadly accepting of the irony. A lament for the unredeemable once-was or might-have-been can be heard in the December wind that blows over Glorious Hill. The faded belle has learned that the possession of time is not, as she had once thought, a gift from heaven, but only a condition for which mortals yearn from their timebound course within the turning years, a beautiful dream to which, like youth, love and innocence, they must inevitably wave goodbye.

The *Eccentricities of a Nightingale* is a simpler script than *Summer and Smoke*. The title refers to the nervous mannerisms of the heroine when speaking, laughing and, in particular, when singing. Yet compared to the Alma of the original play she is not a weak or divided person. She does not debate the issue of body and soul with John. She never refuses him; on the contrary, she pursues him with single-minded aggressiveness. Since he does not love her, she settles for an hour in a hotel with him on New Year's Eve and then turns to casual sex. For his part, John never taunts or derides her. He is not going through a wild phase. There is no Rosa or Papa Gonzales and no Nellie Ewell. Instead of a chiding father, he has a doting mother, who wants her only son to marry well and thinks that Alma would make a poor choice.

The heroine's relatively easy rebellion against her upbringing begins to move the revised playscript back toward the short story. For that matter, the tale of Aunt Albertine, twice told in *Eccentricities* but not once in *Summer and Smoke*, comes from the same vein of wild humour as 'The Yellow Bird'. Alma's psychotic mother (Grace) had a sister (Albertine) who, like herself, was raised in the shadow of the Church. At the turn of the century she ran off in a plumed hat with a twice married (and never divorced) crank (Otto Schwarzkopf) who had created a travelling show of mechanical marvels – drummers, flautists, soldiers and the like – which he called the Musée Mécanique. His favourite invention was a mechanical bird–girl, a wind-up doll that smiled, nodded, and offered its arms in embrace. From its mouth a tin bird popped out every few minutes and sang. Things went well until Schwarzkopf mortgaged the Musée Mécanique to buy a snake that died after swallowing its blanket. Rather than let his creditors sell the Musée, he set fire to it. Albertine ran into the flames to save him but died herself in the attempt.

Like the heroine's ancestor who was hanged for a witch in the short story, the maternal aunt paid the price for rebelling against her puritan heritage. The confessional playwright's admitted identification with the niece who followed her lead strengthens the homosexual hint in the aunt's Proustian name. The mechanical bird–girl with which both Alma and the playwright are identified (Gore Vidal called Williams 'the Bird') was exchanged for the sexually symbolic snake. The heroine gives up singing and begins to pick up men. She uses the plume from her cavalier hat to rouse the fire in the hotel room on the New Year's Eve she spends with John. She says that their one hour will be her lifetime. But, if Albertine's past throws light on Alma's future, the cost of Eden is, as usual, its loss. The devil's emissary, once a chattering bird, next a plunging fish, assumes its familiar serpentine form in the story of the aunt. The appearance of the Nightingale of the Delta in her yellow dress and matching parasol alludes to the legendary Bobo. Its caged frenzy is manifest in the eccentric mannerisms of the singer, its flight in her defiant rebellion.

7
'Cat on a Hot Tin Roof'
(1955)

BRICK POLLITT. Time just outran me, Big Daddy – got there first.

The first production of *Cat on a Hot Tin Roof* opened in 1955 at the Morosco Theatre in New York. It was directed by Elia Kazan with Ben Gazzara as Brick, Barbara Bel Geddes as Margaret, and Burl Ives as Big Daddy. The set and lighting were by Jo Mielziner. The 1958 London production was directed by Peter Hall with Paul Massie as Brick, Kim Stanley as Margaret, and Leo McKern as Big Daddy. The 1958 screen version was written by James Poe and Richard Brooks, and directed by Richard Brooks with Paul Newman, Elizabeth Taylor and Burl Ives. The 1974 New York revival was directed by Michael Kahn with Keir Dullea, Elizabeth Ashley and Fred Gwynne. A television adaptation was produced in 1976 with Robert Wagner, Natalie Wood and Laurence Olivier, and another in 1984 with Tommy Lee Jones, Jessica Lange and Rip Torn.

The story of *Cat on a Hot Tin Roof* begins with Jack

Straw and Peter Ochello, a homosexual couple who in 1910 took in a young vagrant by the name of Pollitt to help them run their cotton plantation in the Mississippi Delta. As the estate grew, Pollitt rose to become overseer, then Ochello's partner after Straw's death, and finally sole owner after Ochello's. At twenty-five he took a wife (Ida), who bore him two sons, eight years apart. He hated the first (Gooper) but loved the second (Brick). By the time they were in college, Pollitt, who had left school at ten, was a multi-millionaire known as Big Daddy to his family, and the plantation stretched over 28,000 acres of rich Delta soil.

The son he hated was a success in the world at thirty-five, the son he loved a has-been at twenty-seven. Gooper became a lawyer, married well and had five children. The handsome Brick, an athletic star in college, became an alcoholic after a short-lived career as a professional football-player and sports announcer. He had taken, reluctantly, a wife of shabby genteel background (Margaret), who held only a lukewarm attraction for him. Even before their marriage he was far more interested in a fellow athlete (Skipper), with whom he imagined he had a 'pure' relationship. When the wife, who soon began to feel like the cat in the title, called the friend to account, he tried to reveal his hidden desire to the husband. Brick would not listen. The rejected Skipper died soon thereafter of drugs and alcohol, and Brick stopped sleeping with Margaret. Holding her responsible for his friend's ruin gave him a reason for no longer engaging in intimacies toward which he had been indifferent from the start.

At about the same time Big Daddy Pollitt stopped sleeping with Ida. In the five-odd years since then he developed terminal cancer. When the play begins, however, he does not yet know the grim prognosis. Indeed, both he and Ida (Big Mama) have been told that, on the contrary, the results of all the recent tests were negative. The enacted events, which are continuous, take place on Big Daddy's birthday in and about the plantation house at which his family have gathered. Gooper, afraid that his father will leave him nothing, has a plan in his briefcase to get control of the estate. Brick, having tried to jump the hurdles at his old high school the previous night, hobbles about on a crutch with one foot in a cast.

In this dramatic elegy the dying father yields his world to the defeated son. Act I shows the non-marriage of the frustrated Margaret and the detached Brick. Act II is the confrontation of Big Daddy and Brick in which the former learns that he is dying and the latter that he is guilty of complicity in the death of his friend for refusing to face the question of homosexuality with him. In Act III Margaret declares that she is pregnant, and, whether or not she can make the lie come true, it is evident that she and Brick will inherit the estate.

There are four published versions of Act III, two of which – the original and the Broadway – are printed in *Theatre*, III (1971) with a note by Williams explaining that the second was written for the premiere production under the prompting of its director, Elia Kazan. In the Broadway version Big Daddy reappears to tell a bawdy joke, thereby showing that he will face death with Pantagruelian equanimity. When Margaret tells him that she is pregnant, he says he wants his lawyer in the morning, proof of confidence that he can now leave his land to his chosen seed. Brick himself shows signs of rehabilitation by openly supporting Margaret in her lie before the suspicious Gooper and his wife (Mae). Perhaps it will come true that very night. When Margaret, having thrown out all the liquor, tells Brick she will get more if he satisfies her desire, he says he admires her. In the play's last moments she kneels at the foot of the bed and vows that she is determined to restore him to life.

In the original version Big Daddy does not reappear. Nor does Brick support Margaret in her lie. But neither does he say anything to put it in question. Big Mama goes to tell her husband the consoling news. We know from her response to it that Brick ('my son, Big Daddy's boy! Little Father!') will be the heir. When Margaret, having locked up the liquor, tells Brick she will take it out again once he satisfies her desire, he says there is nothing to say. In the play's last moments she insists that she loves him, and Brick, in the same phrase his father used when his mother protested as much to her husband, replies, 'Wouldn't it be funny if that was true?' The version used in the 1974 revival is like the original except that Big Daddy reappears to tell his joke. The acting-version is like the Broadway except that the joke is cut.

Although in his *Memoirs* Williams takes pride in *Cat* as a drama of which Aristotle would have approved, no version of Act III quite works, because the final act is an afterthought. Admittedly, the time span is diurnal in *Cat*, as opposed to seasonal in *Menagerie, Summer and Smoke* and *Streetcar*, but this has less to do with Aristotle than with the fact that *Cat* is one of Williams's story-telling plays. It is close in form to *Night of the Iguana*, closer still to the mid-length *Small Craft Warnings*, and closest of all to the better-known mid-length *Suddenly Last Summer*, in which, as in *Cat*, a story (containing the suicide of a young homosexual) is narrated within a dramatic frame that leaves room for the comic relief of a squabble over inheritance by grasping relatives.

The elegiac figure of Big Daddy Pollitt towers over *Cat* like a colossus. The dying of the same light against which he rages, scenic and symbolic, gathers about the legendary old salesman of the Delta in *The Last of my Solid Gold Watches*, Charlie Colton, as he speaks from his heart about the world which has passed him by to his unsympathetic young colleague. In *Cat* Williams again uses the device he perfected in his early one-act plays, that of a character telling his story to poor critical reception. Margaret's long speeches in Act I give an account of herself and her marriage that her husband can barely stand to hear. Big Daddy's earnest performance in Act II prompts his deeply troubled son more than once to stop him. When it is Brick's turn to tell his own story, his father responds by calling him a liar.

Cat is two duologues (I–II) and an ensemble (III). The duologues are essentially monologues. Because the drama is over at the end of the second, the ensemble is an appendage to them. It contains no intrigue because the playwright is interested not in plot but in the revelation of character through confrontation. It contains no suspense because it is a foregone conclusion that the favoured son, a repressed homosexual, will inherit the estate, and another that he will never get over the loss of his youth. In the scene between the hard father and the soft son Williams did everything that he had wanted to do with Brick and Big Daddy. But theatrical convention demanded a longer play, and, as the playwright tells us in his explanatory note, his director asked that Big Daddy not be left out of it, that Margaret be made more sympathetic, and that Brick show some sign of change for the better. According to Peter Hoffman, Williams said that revising Act III to please Kazan 'ruined' him as a writer because it prevented him from dealing honestly with Brick's homosexuality.[1] Yet, while it is true that the Broadway version goes straight for the Happy Ending, the original is only a notch less sentimental and the script of the 1974 revival compromises

112

between the two. When all is said and done, the stage versions are not much more convincing than the screenplay, in which the hero resumes sexual relations with his wife as soon as his problem – that of inadequate paternal love – has been solved by a heart-to-heart talk with his father.

On a deep level, of course, that is just the trouble with Brick. It is because the playwright lacked – or felt he lacked – his father's approval in life that he endowed the favoured son in *Cat* with the attributes of both his male and his female masks. In Brick Pollitt the wanderer and the faded belle begin to coalesce. The 'godlike' ex-football-star, a victim of time under thirty, instead of being a wayfarer is a recluse like Laura Wingfield, to whose physical handicap his present injury corresponds. His alcoholism and his privileged birth ally him with Blanche DuBois. Indeed it is his puritan 'disgust' with homosexuality, no less than Blanche's, that results in the analogous loss by suicide of his closest human tie. Blanche and Brick, as the symbolic white they wear reminds us, had both wished for a kind of marriage of pure souls. The presently withdrawn Brick is a measure of the early Blanche. If her later promiscuity throws further light on the hero, his homosexuality cannot be closeted for long.

As Arthur Ganz has shrewdly observed, what Williams did in *Cat* was to pull *Streetcar* inside out.[2] The beautiful dream of the past appears to unfold in the fabulous reality of the present. Antebellum splendour lost to decadence is regained by paternal endeavour. Instead of a small apartment in an urban slum, we see an enormous bedsitting-room through whose huge double doors a white balustrade indicates the upstairs gallery of a great plantation house. Rather than a hostile exterior encroaching upon a narrow interior, we are confronted by a commodious living-space roofed by the sky and reaching out into a peaceful beyond. Proletarian 'types' are replaced by professional gentlemen, vendors and prostitutes by friendly servants and singing field hands, poker at night with its potential for violence by the leisurely pastime of croquet in the afternoon.

Exposure and eviction, devastating in *Streetcar*, are merely idle threats in *Cat*. It soon becomes obvious that the hero will come into his father's kingdom despite the fertility and chicanery of the comic in-laws. Sexual assault is also reduced to a gesture. At the end of *Streetcar*, the carnal Stanley, dressed in red silk pyjamas, makes Blanche the 'tiger' drop the bottle top and bends her to his will. At the beginning of *Cat*, the celibate Brick, dressed in white silk pyjamas, wards off Maggie the cat's amorous advance by holding a boudoir chair between them like a lion-tamer.

Although in the drama of body and soul the sexes are reversed, it is Big Daddy Pollitt with his physical appetite, rough eloquence and imposing authority who reminds us most of Stanley Kowalski. Both powerful men, adored by their wives, smash through the pretensions of gentility or ritual around them with bare-knuckled realism. But, instead of being the heroine's enemy, Big Daddy is the hero's ally. Whereas in *Streetcar* the rough man ruins the heroine's birthday, in *Cat* he ruins his own – for those about him. He reserves his greatest scorn for his wife, whose pathetic efforts to make the party a success prove vain. Analogously, Margaret fails to get Brick to enter into the spirit of things. Whereas Blanche's present is a notice of eviction, Big Daddy's – all he wanted – is the promise of his favourite son's paternity.

The counterpoint of life and death should seem more hopeful in *Cat*. The removal of Blanche coincides with the appearance of Stella's baby, just as the prognosis of Big

Daddy's death coincides with the announcement of Margaret's pregnancy. In *Streetcar* the birth is a step down, in *Cat* a step up. Stanley's fatherhood is associated with rape, Margaret's motherhood with the outflanking of Mae and Gooper. Whereas in the first case the apes take over, in the second the dogs are held at bay.

Streetcar contemplates an end, *Cat* a beginning. Blanche gives Stanley the bunch of old papers to which debauchery has reduced Belle Reve. Big Daddy gives Brick the Straw and Ochello estate that his own labours have built into a kingdom. Homosexuality is linked to the creation of the plantation instead of to its loss. It is true that in both plays a suicide has aborted a marriage. But the 'degenerate' Allan Grey as the husband of the last DuBois owner belongs to the final phase in a history of slow decay. The 'tender' homosexual love between Jack Straw and Peter Ochello belongs to the initial phase in a history of rapid growth. It is in their very bedroom, moreover, in a setting described as evocative of their benign ghosts, that the present heir, himself a homosexual, is closeted.

Yet, if *Cat* contemplates a beginning, it is the beginning of the end. Big Daddy is dying. The real ruin of the festive occasion is his son's angry announcement to him of the terrible truth that on the anniversary of his birth he must prepare for his death. Nor is Brick likely, despite his protective wife, in his father's house to build more stately mansions. The anxiety of the titular heroine, the result of sexual frustration, already begins to ally her with the faded belle. Her relation to her detached and self-destructive husband is like those in which the belle, or anyhow a character resembling her, tries in vain to save the foredoomed wanderer. There is serious doubt whether the 'frantic' Margaret can keep Brick Pollitt from drinking himself into the grave like his friend Skipper before him.

Margaret drives Brick to drink in 'Three Players of a Summer Game', the short story from which the play derives. There is no Big Daddy and no Skipper, unless the two characters may be said to exist embryonically in the young cancer victim (by the telling name of Grey) with whose widow, Isabel, Brick has a summer affair in the vain attempt to escape from his emasculating wife. The game is croquet, and its three players are Brick, Isabel and her twelve-year-old daughter, Mary Louise, with whom the narrator was friends in the last summer of his childhood. At the end of the story, Williams emphasises the castration theme by comparing Margaret to an ancient conqueror as she drives about town with her amiably senseless husband like a captive in chains behind her. He also defines it by the mortification that the narrator remembers feeling as a boy when Mary Louise lifted the fig leaf off a male nude in a sculpture gallery and, turning to him, asked ingenuously, 'Is yours like that?'

That this incident took place between Williams and Hazel Kramer (it is recorded in his *Memoirs*) reminds us once more of how close the author's psychological life is to his work. What Margaret refers to in *Cat* as Brick's coolness toward sex may ultimately have its root in Williams's fear of castration. Whether it does or not, it is clear that, from an autobiographical standpoint, the play is a wishful fantasy in which Williams receives his father's approval and then kills him. Indeed, he enjoys the preference of both parents over his more worldly brother (a lawyer, like Dakin), whom he turns into a grasper and a fool. He is at the centre of attention by what amounts to natural right: admired while doing nothing to deserve admiration and sexually irresistible while remaining aloof. He creates a friend who commits suicide for the love of him and a wife who says she would do so too if she ever lost hope that he would once more make love to her with the 'indifference' she so rapturously recalls. By making the wife and the friend go to bed together for what Margaret at one point says is the purpose of dreaming of him, the puritan and the cavalier Williams has his cake and eats it too, preserving his goodness while being passionately desired.

The myth of the Old South merges with the longing for a return to spotless childhood in a summer reverie of white and gold. But the longing, like the myth, based on fantasy rather than fact, turns out to be equally vain. Brick is a child in a world of adults, sharing a room, if not a bed, with a maternally protective young woman. He is burdened with the death-like security that Williams says in 'A Streetcar Named Success' came with achieving the 'absolute protection and utter effortlessness' that the 'homesick little boy' in him had always wanted.[3] Significant people and places in the child's dreaming mind – Daddy, Mama, house, plantation – are all big. The late-afternoon sun, filtered through bamboo shades, casts gold-fretted shadows over the big room and across the snowy surface of the big bed that dominates it. A look of benign age, as if of wicker furniture outdoors for many seasons, governs the 'gently and poetically haunted' space where the handsome couple appear in the chaste yet seductive garb of dream life, she in a slip of ivory satin and lace, he in white silk pyjamas.

The child's dream cannot satisfy the man. Nor can the idealistic dream of youth endure beyond life's brief period of bloom. The appearance of the hero with his cast and his crutch defines his role as time's victim. Feelings of immortality and limitless potential have dispersed with the experience of age. Brick's homosexuality and his self-deception regarding it are secondary to his discovery that the 'dream of life' is over. He drinks, he tells his father, because he no longer 'believes'. The end of the romance of his friendship and the end of his athletic career have taught him that he is neither a 'pure' nor an ageless being but a creature of frail flesh already defeated in the futile race with time.

The first production stressed the play's dreamlike quality. On walking into the Morosco theatre, one noticed the point or corner of a raked platform extending past the scrim at the proscenium line, sloping down over the pit like the prow of a plunging ship, and reaching into the house itself, where the first two rows of orchestra seats had been replaced by settees. There was no curtain. When the house lights dimmed, horizontal bars of alternating light and shade were projected on the scrim from the balcony rail. As the first words were spoken, upstage lighting faded in to reveal Jo Mielziner's full set: an enormous room with soaring jalousies at the far end that the projections on the transparent scrim, which was now slowly opening, had suggested. There were no walls or doors. An ornate fresco with two plump cupids decorated the floating canopy above.[4] A catwalk suggested a balcony outside the windows. The console liquor cabinet was up left. The bed was up centre, its high wicker headboard twisted into an elaborate cornucopia motif.

In the beginning, shifting clouds and shadows, later stars and fireworks, were visible through the open jalousies, projected images on a cyclorama under which mirroring suggested the surface of an adjacent pond or stream. A gauze curtain in front of the cyclorama enhanced the illusion of depth. In the code phrase of Century Lighting, which supplied the equipment for the production, the scenes were 'painted with light'. The sunset colours with which Act I began gave way to the pale moonlight of Act III.

During key scenes the general lighting was dimmed or even turned out completely as actors worked in follow spots trained on them from the balcony.

Elia Kazan's ceremonial blocking was part of the anti-naturalistic conception. Actors changed position like figures in a drill and stood in formal groups as if posing for pictures. They sometimes held position for as long as ten beats. These effects made perceptive critics such as Eric Bentley and Henry Hewes think of film.[5] The arrested action was analogous to the freeze frame just as the follow spot was to the close-up. Despite the audacious theatricality of the set, lighting and directing, the acting of individual roles was marked by the detail and intensity of the neo-Stanislavskyan American Method. Ben Gazzara's sullen, mumbling Brick was within the Actors Studio tradition established by Marlon Brando's Stanley Kowalski. Barbara Bel Geddes's golden Margaret matched in sincerity his deep concentration. The corpulent Burl Ives, best known as a folk singer, gave to the profane, waggish and wrathful Big Daddy the appearance of solid reality.

If truth to nature lay just under the deliberate artifice of the performance, the teeming life of the plantation lay just outside the magical space defined by the raked stage. The prompt-book for *Cat*, according to its production stage-manager, was 'a veritable scenario' of off-stage footsteps, birdcalls, songs and conversation.[6] From time to time the blues of Brownie McGhee on guitar and Sonny Terry on harmonica could be heard faintly in the distance. The effect of the whole suggested the experience of the mind while in the condition of reverie when the events of the real world seem to lie just beyond the symbolic visions that float up from the unconscious.

The problem of playing *Cat* in 1955 was how much to

make of Brick's homosexuality. The result was equivocation. That is why several critics were dissatisfied with the inconclusiveness of Ben Gazzara's Brick and what appeared to be his miraculous 'salvation' by Barbara Bel Geddes's shimmering Margaret. Watts of the *New York Post* had great trouble believing the happy conclusion. Eric Bentley blamed the director. Kerr of the *New York Herald-Tribune* took Williams to task for not making Brick's motives clear. Yet Kerr, reviewing the 1974 revival for the *New York Times*, complimented the playwright with having known what he was about all along. It only took Keir Dullea's hysterical outbursts to show that the hero was protesting his virility too much. Elizabeth Ashley, furthermore, by stressing Margaret's feline tenacity, held the character back from the trap of sentimentality.

The problem of playing *Cat* today would be how to subordinate the dated topic of homosexuality to the perennial and overriding subject of loss in time. The key is the hero's likeness to his father. The reason for Brick's favoured position as 'son of Big Daddy' is that both men are close in spirit to an earlier and simpler America, or at least to the romance of one. The great self-made planter and the ex-football idol are out of place in the modern corporate nation. The present belongs to the Goopers. The age of heroes is past. The plantation version of the agrarian myth thereby serves the elegiac theme. The action of the play is the passing of the father and the passing of the youth of the son. The father's end is near, the son's beginning is over. Brick, having peaked, has begun the slow process of dying which, in the playwright's view, constitutes the remainder of human life and demonstrates nature's passion for declivity.

8
Wanderer Plays (1957–9)

ALEXANDRA DEL LAGO. All day I've kept hearing a sort
of lament that drifts through the air of this place. It
says, 'Lost, lost, never to be found again'. (*Sweet
Bird of Youth*)

The wanderer plays of the late 1950s complement the great
faded-belle plays of the late 1940s. Between the two
groups stands the pivotal *Cat on a Hot Tin Roof* (1955), in
which Williams endowed the focal character of Brick Pollitt
with attributes from each of the twin archetypes. After the
success of *Cat* it was logical for the playwright to turn
seriously to the matter of the wanderer with the intention of
raising it to the level to which he had already brought the
matter of the faded belle.

The paradigmatic wanderer play is a grim threnody for
lost youth, love and art called *Orpheus Descending*. The
first (1957) Broadway production was directed by Harold
Clurman with Cliff Robertson as Val, Maureen Stapleton
as Lady, and Lois Smith as Carol. The 1960 film

adaptation, called *The Fugitive Kind*, was written by Williams and Meade Roberts, and directed by Sidney Lumet with Marlon Brando as Val, Anna Magnani as Lady, Maureen Stapleton as Vee, and Joanne Woodward as Carol.

The handsome hero of *Orpheus*, Valentine Xavier, is putatively an itinerant folk singer. Wearing his snakeskin jacket and carrying his guitar, Val comes on his thirtieth birthday to a small town in rural Mississippi where he manages to get a job as a shoe salesman in a general store. As his name suggests, he is both saviour and Valentine, a male sex object to whom the women of the play turn for salvation. Vee Talbott, a painter and religious visionary, confuses him with Christ. Carol Cutrere, a disillusioned reformer of aristocratic family, wants him to run away with her. But he attaches himself to Lady Torrance, the storekeeper's wife, an older woman who becomes pregnant by him. On the day before Easter she is shot by her husband, Jabe, and Val is lynched by the angry townsmen.

The setting for these baleful events is an ominously non-realistic evocation of the store. Strips of flypaper attach to the motionless fan that hangs from the inordinately high ceiling under which, on the upstage wall, a huge window looks out onto a bleak landscape. Bolts of fabric, shelves of shoe boxes, and a dressmaker's dummy in front of a thin white column are all that suggest merchandise. A staircase leads to the second-floor living-quarters past a landing with a 'sinister-looking' artificial palm. There are two incongruous areas. One is the tiny downstairs bedroom where Val sleeps, an alcove whose translucent curtain is adorned by a gold tree with scarlet fruit and white birds. The other is the redecorated 'confectionary', scheduled to open for drinks on the night of the killings, a partly visible room whose wind chimes, silver stars, Christmas lights and paper branches represent Lady's effort to re-create the lost garden café of her father, an Italian immigrant, who died in the fire when the Mystic Crew destroyed his orchards because he had broken the racial code by serving black customers.

Several layers of symbolism, principally seasonal, Greek and Christian, labour the themes of *Orpheus Descending*. Val's story alludes to the fate of the poet–singer of Greek myth who failed to bring back his beloved Eurydice from the kingdom of the dead and was torn apart by a band of fierce Maenads. If Val is Orpheus, then the fearful Jabe, now terminally ill, who boasts he led the gang that killed Lady's father long ago, is clearly Hades. The symbolic labels advertise the conflicts between life and death, love and hatred, art and nature, and flesh and spirit that crowd the play. The strange figure of Uncle Pleasant (Conjure Man) with his Choctaw cry and his charms and talismans of shell, bone, and feather, appears to support the Calvinist view of spiritual purity *versus* fleshly corruption, and at the same time to suggest that despite the spread of commerce there is still something wild in the country.

The lynching of Val Xavier – saint, saviour, son of Apollo – is like the death of a god. He is an elegiac figure, tarnished by corruption but uncorrupted, as his guitar and snakeskin jacket, badges of purity in art and nature, clearly indicate. He looks back to the days before he became a male prostitute, when as a child on Witch's Bayou he survived alone by hunting and fishing, and further back, before his family scattered like feathers in the wind, to his origin in a higher realm with strongly Wordsworthian intimations. Val, who would like to have been a bird that never lights upon the surly earth, describes the loss of his Belle Reve in a song, 'Heavenly Grass', one of the Blue Mountain ballads from Williams's first collection of poems:

123

My feet took a walk in heavenly grass.
All day while the sky shone clear as glass.
My feet took a walk in heavenly grass,
All night while the lonesome stars rolled past.
Then my feet came down to walk on earth,
And my mother cried when she gave me birth.
Now my feet walk far and my feet walk fast,
But they still got an itch for heavenly grass.
But they still got an itch for heavenly grass.[1]

Actually, *Orpheus* is a revision of *Battle of Angels* (1940), which closed in Boston without coming to New York. In the early version the plot is looser, the cast is larger, and the symbolism more intrusive. Val is an aspiring writer instead of a musician. His death is precipitated by the appearance of a woman he spurned who in retaliation has followed him from Texas to charge him with rape. The antagonism of the townsmen toward him begins when he saves a homeless black man (Loon) from the charge of vagrancy. Carol Cutrere (called Cassandra Whiteside) serves as a prophetess whose urgent promptings to escape with her Val fails to heed. Lady (called Myra) has no Italian father nor does she plan to reopen a confectionary. The play is framed by a prologue and an epilogue during which tourists, a year after the action, are escorted through the old Torrance store (now a museum) by two guides whose names (they are the Temple sisters) insist upon the religious significance of the drama no less than does the title itself.

In 1958, the year following *Orpheus*, the mid-length *Suddenly Last Summer* opened off Broadway with the one-act *Something Unspoken* in a double bill entitled *Garden District*. The plays were directed by Herbert Machiz with Anne Meacham as Catharine, Hortense

Alden as Mrs Venable, and Robert Lansing as Dr
Cuckrowicz in *Suddenly*, and Eleanor Phelps as Cornelia
and Hortense Alden as Grace in *Something Unspoken*. The
1959 film version of *Suddenly*, written by Williams and
Gore Vidal, was directed by Joseph Mankiewicz with
Elizabeth Taylor as Catharine, Katherine Hepburn as Mrs
Venable, and Montgomery Clift as Dr Cuckrowicz.

Although the wanderer does not appear in *Suddenly*, he
is nevertheless the focal character. Sebastian Venable, the
rich, handsome, forty-year-old but still youthful-looking
poet, pederast and world-traveller, is eaten alive by a gang
of beach urchins in a faraway country. The story comes to
light during the psychiatric examination of his young cousin
Catharine Holly, who replaced his mother as his travelling-
companion and procuress during the last summer of his life.
Evidently Sebastian, who had never written more than one
poem a year, suddenly felt old, stopped writing completely,
and submitted himself to death. His mother, an aging New
Orleans belle, who recalls with pride that she and her son
were 'a famous couple', would like the handsome young
doctor in the play to perform a lobotomy on Catharine in
order to cut the scandalous story from her brain.

At the curtain Catharine's fate remains somewhat in
doubt. But it is clear that Sebastian's punishment fits his
crime of purchasing children's flesh to satisfy his sexual
appetite. The Darwinian view of nature red in tooth and
claw also lies behind the wish to sacrifice himself to the
cruel god whose face he had seen, while sailing the
Encantadas long ago, behind the spectacle of carnivorous
birds swooping down upon the newly hatched sea turtles as
they tried desperately to reach the safety of the water. 'Eat
and be eaten' is the law of both sex and survival in this
bizarre play, as the Venus flytrap, among other rare and
frightening growths in the garden of the Venable residence,

plainly indicates. Massive tree flowers seem to glisten with undried blood like the organs of a body, torn out. Ominous cries, hissings and thrashing sounds continually punctuate the dialogue.

The botanical and zoological metaphor extends to the names of people and places. The predatory mother, Violet Venable ('venery' means both lust and hunting), would trap and destroy her niece, an offspring of the Holly family. The specialist from Lion's View is to root out of the victim the living memory of Cabeza de Lobo (Wolf's Head), a name that puns on the surgical procedure in question. Violet's paid companion, Miss Foxhill, helps in the effort to win over Dr Cuckrowicz (from the Polish for sugar) whose appetising good looks are lost on neither the mother, who warms to him flirtatiously, nor her niece, who assaults him with the tenacity of a hungry bear cub.

The contest between Violet and Catharine over Dr Sugar continues the sexual rivalry between them that began over Sebastian. Indeed the lobotomist, with his glacial brilliance and icy charm, bears a striking resemblance to the elegant and ruthless poet. The white-on-white figure of the doctor, a blond man 'all in white', reflects that of the wandering writer in his white suit, white hat, white tie and lizard-skin pumps, who died against a white wall near a white beach on a blazing white day. To provide his audience with a glimpse of the focal character, Williams makes the living man incarnate the dead.

Suddenly was paired with *Something Unspoken* in 1958 because of the setting of both plays within the affluent garden district of New Orleans. The one-act play is an ostensibly comic duologue between a wealthy clubwoman (Cornelia Scott) and her poor companion–secretary (Grace Lancaster) in the course of which Cornelia learns that she has failed to be nominated for Regent of the

Confederate Daughters. What is unspoken between the two women is not only rivalry and sexual attraction but also the mutual dread that the present has nothing to offer. The pliant Grace is a faded belle, a homeless widow with the memory of a lost love. The domineering Cornelia, whose name feminises the playwright's father's, is an obsolete dinosaur in a world that has passed her by, an anachronism whose only pride is her ancestry. Despite its comic veneer, *Something Unspoken* finally expounds the sad and familiar theme of time's decay.

In 1959, the year after *Garden District*, the first Broadway production of *Sweet Bird of Youth* was directed by Elia Kazan with Paul Newman as Chance and Geraldine Page as Alexandra, who repeated their roles in the 1962 film adaptation written and directed by Richard Brooks. The sacrificial figure of the wanderer, dressed in white silk pyjamas, appears in *Sweet Bird* as the hapless Chance Wayne. Like Val and Sebastian, Chance is a kind of itinerant artist who attaches himself to an older woman. The would-be actor, still lean and handsome at twenty-nine despite his thinning hair and ravaged face (he has survived as a beach boy and gigolo for years), returns as the paramour of the fading movie star Alexandra Del Lago to his hometown of St Cloud in pursuit of his long cherished hopes – a career in pictures and reunion with his first love, Heavenly Finley. But Heavenly is unattainable and Alexandra can be neither bribed nor persuaded to help him. His fate is to be castrated on Easter Sunday. Time is the enemy of us all, says Chance, in a curtain speech that sums up his role as a might-have-been whose luck ran out despite his celestial headstart in this dramatic elegy for the lost dreams of youth.

Sweet Bird is an expansion of *The Enemy: Time* (written in 1952), a one-act play that consists primarily of a duologue between the hero and his first love during which a grandfather clock with smiling moon face may be heard ticking loudly in the background. At the end he is beaten up by the brother of his old sweetheart and left writhing on the ground by the fading movie star, who only comes on to scold him. Williams expanded the one-act into the full-length play by building up the part of the actress and adding an element of social protest. Heavenly's father is the corrupt and reactionary politician Boss Finley, whose thugs are about to castrate Chance at the curtain just as they, or others like them, had earlier castrated a black man as a warning against the threat of miscegenation. The black man's only wrong was to be found on the streets of the state capital at night. Chance's was to give Heavenly a venereal disease whose cure required an ovariectomy. His punishment, therefore, like Sebastian Venable's, fits his crime.

There are five castrations in *Sweet Bird*, three real and two metaphorical. Chance tells Alexandra that his position as her paid prostitute has 'castrated' him. The actress replies that age does the same thing to a woman. She has been travelling with him under the name of the Princess Kosmonopolis in the effort to escape from what she believes to have been the fiasco of her attempt to return to the screen. The success of her comeback contrasts with the failure of Chance's homecoming. Nevertheless, the heroine's crisis, like the hero's, serves the theme of eroding time through the uneven contest of life with death and of art with grim reality. Although Alexandra takes pride in climbing the beanstalk, she admits she has become a monster to do so, a role for which she is by no means typecast, as we know from her compassion for Chance. Her false name, with its intimations of worldly power, cannot shield her genuine vulnerability. Her star is falling, a fact of which the surprisingly good response to her film can no more numb her awareness for long than the sex, drugs and alcohol that have failed to do so since her flight in panic from the screening. Her chances too have waned.

The real ruler of Beanstalk Country is not the make-believe Princess, Kosmonopolis, but the political monster, Boss Finley. His daughter is mortgaged to the surgeon who operated on her at the hospital her father built. His henchman evicts Chance and Alexandra from their hotel. His image fills the stage's rear wall during his speech at a political rally. In the theatrical *tour de force* that ends Act II, Chance looks frontwards into a flickering spot as if the television screen were at the balcony rail as, simultaneously, the gigantic figure of the Boss looms over the darkened stage and somewhere an unseen heckler is beaten.

The rally illustrates the openness of *Sweet Bird* as opposed to the confinement of *Orpheus*, paralleling the contrast between *Streetcar* and *Summer and Smoke*. The shabby mercantile store, with its cobwebbed walls and dusty window, gives way to the arches, door frames, and balustrades that indicate, against a cyclorama of sea, sky and royal palms, the multiple locations of the play. The occasional cry of birds and the constant sighing of the wind, sometimes merging with a thematic music called 'The Lament' in the stage directions, help to create a wistful, elegiac sense of place despite the violence of events.

Williams's archetypal actions, the eviction and the spoiled occasion, make up the climax both of *Orpheus* and of *Sweet Bird*. Sheriff Talbott warns Val to leave the county, and Boss Finley, through his agents, warns Chance to leave town. The spoiled occasion is not only the failure of Lady's confectionary to open or of Chance's homecoming to be the celebration he had wished. It is also the desecration of that holiday in the Christian calendar which

129

marks the Resurrection with its promise of renewal and redemption. A special combination of sex, religiosity and death (or at least the stoppage of future life) creates the world of the wanderer plays as it does that of the wanderer stories, 'The Malediction', 'The Poet', 'One Arm' and 'Desire and the Black Masseur'. The pun in the last-mentioned title shows that Williams was toying with the idea of the Black Mass. The central figure of the two full-length plays is a male sex object with divine or angelic attributes whose destiny, like that of Anthony Burns, is to be sacrificed in a blasphemous inversion of Holy Saturday or Easter Sunday.

The death of Sebastian Venable in the mid-length *Suddenly* is an indirect allusion to the Eucharist. Williams, who entered psychoanalysis in 1957, presents the atavistic act of killing by eating as if to suggest the slaying of the primeval father which Freud made a cornerstone of psychoanalytic theory in *Totem and Taboo* and *Moses and Monotheism*. As described by Catharine, the cannibalising of Sebastian (performed to primitive music) illustrates Freud's view of the origin of the totem feast and the symbolic re-enactment of that rite in the Christian Communion.

Of even greater significance is the figure of St Sebastian himself, by tradition a beautiful youth who was loved by the emperor Diocletian until Sebastian's conversion to Christianity. The consequent execution of the saint by arrows was a frequent subject of Italian Renaissance painting, as it is in fact of Williams's poem 'San Sebastiano de Sodoma'.[2] A picture representing the martyrdom hangs on the wall of Sebastian Venable's room in the film version of the play. Williams's choice of the saint's name (it was Oscar Wilde's too after his release from jail) gives the death of his wandering poet an immediate religious and sexual meaning. The conflation of images that results from the penetration of the martyr's flesh in death and in sex suggests an experience of simultaneous agony and ecstasy like the transverberation of St Teresa de Ávila as her heart is pierced by an angel's fiery arrow in the famous Bernini altarpiece.

The fusion of death, sex and religiosity in what might be called the St Sebastian syndrome implies that the relationship of Val and Lady or of Chance and Alexandra goes beyond adultery and prostitution into the homosexuality and incest virtually explicit in the case of Sebastian and Violet. In so far as the older women are mothers or mother surrogates, the Oedipal wanderer's terrible punishment is no more than he fears he deserves. On the other hand, in so far as the heroines are the playwright himself, the golden youths are sex partners who take upon themselves the sins of their creator. From this point of view, the tormented Sebastian died for the possessive Violet, Val died for Lady, and Chance was emasculated so that Alexandra could climb the beanstalk once more. The wanderer's doom, accordingly, precludes redemption because he is no mere sinner but a rebel angel who professes the sacred causes of love and art. However, since in Williams those causes are part and parcel of the romance of youth, they are fated to be lost in unforgiving time. The major wanderer plays show the author in his forties reaching in vain for the elusive bird of younger days, for the salvation of forbidden love, and for the lost poetry that – as Violet Venable would put it – seemed once to have been synonymous with life.

9
Reversals of the Pattern
(1943–61)

ASSUNTA. Tick, tick, tick, tick. – You say the clock is a
    liar.
SERAFINA. No, the clock is a fool. I don't listen to it. My
    clock is my heart and my heart don't say tick-
    tick.   (*The Rose Tattoo*)

Scattered over the course of Williams's long career are a
number of plays and stories in which the faded belle or the
wanderer is not defeated. They are nearly all comedies,
inclining toward the farcical, the fantastic or the brazenly
romantic, whose heroes and heroines represent inversions
of the two archetypal figures. Dorothy Simple in *The Case
of the Crushed Petunias* and Kilroy in *Ten Blocks on the
Camino Real* show the principle already at work among the
early one-act plays. Gewinner Pearce in *The Knightly
Quest* and Alma Tutwiler in *The Yellow Bird* manifest
it in the fiction. The major examples from the full-length
plays are Serafina Delle Rose in *The Rose Tattoo* (1950),
Kilroy in *Camino Real* (1953) and Hannah Jelkes in *The

Night of the Iguana (1961). In the first, a broad comedy, we see the triumph of the faded belle; in the second, an extravaganza, that of the wanderer; and in the third, a deeply elegiac play, that of an androgynous character who, like Brick Pollitt, combines aspects of the two. At the beginning of the 1950s, therefore, Williams wrote the comic antithesis of each of his personal myths, and at the beginning of the 1960s a serious answer to both.

It is not surprising that he turned to the faded belle first, since he had been concentrating on the matter of the belle in the late 1940s. Even before *The Glass Menagerie* he had collaborated on a play whose heroine is the happy counterpart of Laura Wingfield. Matilda Rockley is a sexually withdrawn young woman who spends her time polishing silver (instead of glass figurines) in *You Touched Me!* (1943), a romantic comedy written with Donald Windham and based on D. H. Lawrences's short story of the same name. The scene is the interior of a repressively Victorian English country house to which Matilda's gentleman caller arrives, like Laura's, full of energy and forward-looking notions. But he does not disappoint her by already being engaged. The dashing suitor sweeps the shy damsel off her feet, out of the house and away to a bold new future.

That she has no future is the assumption behind the voluntary withdrawal from life of Serafina Delle Rose, the middle-aged but still voluptuous little widow of *The Rose Tattoo*, the first production of which opened in Chicago in 1950 and in New York the following year. It was directed by Daniel Mann with Maureen Stapleton as Serafina and Eli Wallach as Alvaro. The 1955 film was written by Williams, adapted by Hal Kanter, and directed by Daniel Mann with Anna Magnani as Serafina and Burt Lancaster as Alvaro.

Like *You Touched Me!* the play is built on a comic

reversal of the *Menagerie* pattern. As a Williams faded belle, Serafina looks back with longing to a past of erotic fulfilment and 'aristocratic' connections. She is entitled to be addressed as 'baronessa' because her dead husband, who worked for gangsters, had been born in Sicily into a family of small landowners. She cannot believe the two floozies (they reappear eight years later in the one-act *A Perfect Analysis Given by a Parrot*) who take malicious pleasure in informing her that he was unfaithful. She so idolises him that, having withdrawn herself from sex for the three years since his death, she now attempts to withdraw her daughter (Rosa) from it as well. Her ambition for Rosa reverses that of Amanda for Laura. Both mothers fail; but, whereas the hospitable Amanda fails to marry off the retiring Laura, the reclusive Serafina fails to hold back the spirited Rosa. By the end of the play, the daughter leaves to spend the night with her sailor boyfriend. The mother, finally convinced of her husband's infidelity, smashes his urn and takes another man.

Palm trees, tall cane and pampas grass dress the stage, giving a feeling of almost tropical warmth to the little Gulf-coast village that provides the play's setting. A goat runs loose and children scamper with kites and hoops in front of the rude frame cottage where Serafina takes in washing while truckloads of phallic bananas roar by on the highway above. The dead husband had driven a truck, and so does his replacement, Alvaro Mangiacavallo, whose name ('Eat-a-horse') contributes to the plant and animal imagery and alludes to the playwright's lover, Frank Merlo, to whom the play is dedicated, and for whom Williams's nickname was 'Little Horse'.[1] At the curtain rise, coloured lights, reminding us of those under whose stimulus Stanley and Stella Kowalski were wont to make love, twinkle against the blue sky of the *prima sera* like reflections on the water of a harbour at evening.

The comedy bubbles over with the puckish spirit of sex. The flower after which the author's sister was named is both primary symbol and running gag. The heroine is discovered with a rose in her hair, sitting against a backdrop of rose wallpaper, a bowl of roses nearby, as she waits for her husband, Rosario Delle Rose, who combs his hair with rose oil, to return. Their daughter, Rosa, was conceived on the extraordinary night that the rose tattoo on Rosario's chest was duplicated upon Serafina's. Within the cottage, two dressmaker's dummies, one draped for a widow, the other a bride, stand in attitudes of contention to assert the conflict of Thanatos and Eros. The latter's easy triumph in *The Rose Tattoo* shows the elegiac Williams looking through rose-coloured glasses.

His two archetypal actions are accordingly reversed. Instead of an eviction, there is a breaking-free. The cherished shrine to Rosario, false testimony to the dead past, must no longer confine the living present. Nor may the occasion of Rosa's high-school graduation be spoiled by her overly anxious mother. On the contrary, its festive spirit is carried home to the very hearth of the kill-joy. Serafina, who at first forbids Rosa to attend the ceremonies, at last relents. The girls get their dresses just in time. When later the new graduate, full of the day's excitement, returns with her diploma, her prize and her boyfriend, even the troubled heroine starts to get in the mood.

In her confusion, she forgets to give Rosa her present. But it is only a watch that does not work; nor would it matter if it did. Serafina declares early in the play that the clock is a fool who says 'tick-tick', while her heart says 'love-love'. The victory of love over time is continuous with that of life over death in the comic 'resurrection' of the dead husband. Alvaro has a clown's face but Rosario's body. To woo the widow, he gets a rose tattoo, which is duplicated upon her the night they make love just as Alvaro's had been long ago. Not surprisingly, she becomes pregnant again, or anyhow she thinks she does. Thus the miracle of resurrection, denied by the ruined Easters of *Orpheus* and *Sweet Bird*, receives in Williams's satyr play, *The Rose Tattoo*, an exuberant affirmation.

An even wilder treatment of the resurrection idea may be seen three years later in *Camino Real*, a work based on a comic reversal of the wanderer pattern. The first Broadway production was directed by Elia Kazan in 1953 with Eli Wallach as Kilroy, Jo Van Fleet as Marguerite, Joseph Anthony as Casanova, and Hurd Hatfield as Byron. Williams's inspiration for the hero (Kilroy) was the legendary GI of the Second World War who had been everywhere and gone, a creation of the whimsical and ubiquitous graffito 'Kilroy was here'. He appears in *Camino* as an innocent abroad, a has-been boxer who is robbed, rejected, and ridiculed from his arrival by freighter at an alien shore until his departure on foot for yet other lands unknown.

The play is set in a fantastic, Casablanca-like seaport meant to symbolise the crossroads between the royal and the real paths of life, as the Spanish *versus* the English pronunciation of the title implies. The luxury hotel, Siete Mares, looks out across a central plaza to the flophouse, Ritz Men Only, with its adjacent pawnshop and gypsy's stall. No water runs in the plaza fountain because the spring of humanity has gone dry here. The only birds are those that are kept in cages. Since the royal road is a dream of past youth and the real road is a view of present age, the most conspicuous characters among the transients are beautiful people from history and literature transformed into has-beens. Casanova is an old lover, Camille is a faded courtesan, and Byron is a wayward idealist who has philandered too long in Italy. The essential condition of homelessness extends beyond the vagrant Kilroy and the penniless Casanova to all who stop at this port of entry and departure on their journey through life in time. Their response, ordinarily, is a form of self-pity or withdrawal. The sad Casanova must depend for solace upon the barely willing Camille. Lady Mulligan, the tycoon's wife, escapes on an unscheduled flight of the symbolic *Fugitivo*. Others die. Only three out of many have the courage to set forth upon 'Terra Incognita', the wasteland beyond the town's ancient walls. One is Kilroy, the roving victim. One is Byron, the wandering poet. The third is Don Quixote, the errant knight, in whose dream the play's action for the most part occurs.

During its course the hero experiences two 'resurrections'. The first is a symbolic rejuvenation in a spring carnival that Williams describes as derivative of pagan fertility rites. The crowds celebrate Kilroy as the lover and champion of his earlier days. But he is really a dupe. His youth is no more recoverable than is the virginity of Esmeralda, the gypsy's daughter, who proclaims him the carnival's 'Chosen Hero' as a means of luring him to her stall. The carnival is the spoiled occasion or ruined festivity of *Camino*, analogous to the desecrated Easters of the wanderer group. The second resurrection comes at the end after the hero's 'real' death. Having been removed by the sinister Streetcleaners, mourned by the Madrecita, and even partly dismembered by the Medical Instructor, the irrepressible Kilroy springs back into life and runs away with the golden heart that has only just been cut out of his chest.

Kilroy's golden heart and golden gloves help to identify him with Byron and Don Quixote as a version of Williams's archetypal wanderer. His heart denotes his innate purity, his gloves his former glory. Byron, whose character is the play's major addition to the one-act *Ten Blocks on the Camino Real*, from which it derives, embarks on a voyage to discover himself as he once was, counselling others to do likewise; but we know that for all his brave words he will soon die in Greece. The lame foot of the handsome and athletic poet corresponds to the abnormal heart (enlarged as well as golden) of the former champion. Before leaving on his final voyage, Byron gives a harrowing account of the cremation of another wandering poet, Shelley, drowned at thirty, and remarks in a recurrent Williams phrase on 'the passion for declivity in this world'.[2]

At the end of *Camino Real*, Don Quixote awakes from his dream and continues his brave march into stern reality clothed in the armour of his romantic faith. Kilroy joins forces with him, leaving his heart behind in the same shop where he had earlier pawned his gloves. The hero's exit as Sancho Panza's replacement accords with his conception as a comic variant of the defeated wanderer. His cartoon-like resurrection after the excision of his heart by the doctor is the farcical denial of Shelley's decomposition after the removal of his heart from the crematorial fire by his friend Trelawny. The triumph of the impossible is, so to speak, mad as Don Quixote, whose cavalier plume reminds us less of Cyrano de Bergerac's than it does of the white scarf of Gewinner Pearce as he soars on a spaceship to nowhere at the end of *The Knightly Quest*. The spring flows again in the plaza fountain when Kilroy departs with the indomitable Don. Still, if the face of the painted phoenix in the window of the Siete Mares were more plainly visible, we should probably find that it was winking.

Reversals of the Pattern

In *Period of Adjustment* (1960) Williams returned to the classic comic subject of Eros triumphant upon which he had written *The Rose Tattoo* a decade earlier. The first Broadway production was directed by George Roy Hill with Barbara Baxley as Isabel and Robert Webber as George. The 1962 film was writen by Richard Brooks and directed by George Roy Hill with Jane Fonda as Isabel and Jim Hutton as George. The heroine, a pretty newlywed (Isabel Haverstick) whose ladylike manners and shrill delivery align her with Blanche DuBois and Alma Winemiller, comes to terms with marriage, as does her husband (George Haverstick) and the other couple who spend Christmas Eve with them in a bungalow in the South where the play is set. If the women must put aside their romantic expectations, the men must forgo their dreams of adventure. An on-stage television set tuned to a Western provides a popular version of the agrarian myth of America as a thematic backdrop to the husbands' nostalgic war reminiscences and talk of becoming Texas ranchers. The play's subtitle, *High Point over a Cavern* (the bungalow sinks into an underground abyss a little more each year), suggests the eviction or loss-of-home theme so common in Williams and makes clear the elegiac premise of this 'serious comedy' that giving up the beautiful dream of youth for the mundane reality of middle age is a necessary adjustment whose period is but a moment in a gradual process of decline.

That decline is treated less trivially in *The Night of the Iguana* (1961). The first Broadway production was directed by Frank Corsaro with Patrick O'Neal as Shannon, Bette Davis as Maxine, Margaret Leighton as Hannah, and Alan Webb as Nonno. The 1964 film was written by Anthony Veiller and directed by John Huston with Richard Burton as Shannon, Ava Gardner as Maxine, and Deborah Kerr as

Hannah. The acceptance of death and transience within a play that does not invoke the licence of comedy to mitigate such conditions makes *Iguana* an exception within the canon. An autumnal tone governs this dramatic elegy. Yet home-finding, fortitude and fulfilment reverse the eviction, derangement and sacrifice with which the belle and wanderer patterns typically conclude.

Williams's archetypes coalesce in each of *Iguana*'s two main characters much as they do in the hero of *Cat*. The alcoholic and neurasthenic T. Lawrence Shannon is a handsome thirty-five-year-old former priest who has lost his faith and acquired a reputation for lechery. Now earning his living as a tour guide, he brings a group of female schoolteachers to the run-down seaside hotel in Mexico where the play is set. Hannah Jelkes (the similar names 'Hannah' and 'Shannon' already suggest an affinity) is an early-middle-aged artist of androgynous appearance and saintly nature who has been following a life of refined vagrancy with her grandfather, Jonathan Coffin (Nonno), a nonagenarian poet. They have moved from one hotel to another for years, paying their way with poetry recitations and quick portrait sketches in charcoal or watercolour. The night is one of trial not only for the three wanderers but also for the giant lizard that the Mexican boys have tied under the hotel verandah to torture, kill and eat. The old poet dies before morning after finishing his last verse. Shannon, having been fired from his job, sets the iguana free and takes the offer of the recently widowed hotel proprietress (Maxine Faulk) to remain with her. Hannah, destitute and alone, endures her fate with quiet fortitude, as the orange tree in Nonno's final poem suffers without a cry or a prayer the change of days and seasons.

Shannon's past in the Episcopal Church and his present in sexual scandal (he first loses his parish and later his tour group for having sexual relations with teenage girls) corresponds to the origin of Valentine Xavier and Chance Wayne in a symbolic heaven and their end in a world of sin and pain. His entrapment between the contrary demands of flesh and spirit corresponds to the dilemma of Alma Winemiller and Blanche DuBois, with whom he shares the heritage of a genteel or even a distinguished Southern family as well as a nervous condition, bordering on psychosis, for which he has twice been institutionalised.

There is no Shannon in the short story of the same name from which the play comes. It is the faded belle (her name is Edith instead of Hannah) who has suffered a nervous breakdown. As a result, she has had to give up her post as art teacher in an Episcopal school for girls and has since been travelling on the small inheritance she receives as the descendant of a once prominent Southern family. Finding herself at a small Mexican hotel out of season, Edith manages to relieve her loneliness by forcing her company upon two homosexual writers, the younger of whom releases the iguana tied under the verandah while the elder, despite her protests, reaches orgasm by sexually assaulting her. When writing the play, Williams transferred some of Edith's attributes to the new character of Shannon. Partly by way of compensation, he obscured the gender of the heroine, made her a New Englander and added the familiar wandering poet, now aged ninety-seven, as her close blood relation and travelling-companion. Hannah says that she and her grandfather have made their homes in one another, a telling statement which, in view of Maxine's having told them that they must leave in the morning, lessens – at least for the moment – the severity of the eviction theme.

Not even Nonno's death in the night results in the life-maiming heartbreak for which the belle is ordinarily destined. It is not the heroine's loneliness but the hero's shattered nerves that are in need of remedy, a need that is served, moreover, not by furtive sex but by honesty and compassion. Hannah easily withstands the overtures of Shannon, who has been tied in a hammock after his declared intention to drown himself. His self-pitying histrionics, continuous with his suicide gesture, lead Hannah to call him to account for imagining that he can atone for the sins of the world by indulging in a kind of 'voluptuous crucifixion' without nails on a hill far lovelier than Golgotha. The allusion to Good Friday corresponds to the Holy Saturday on which Val Xavier is lynched and the Easter Sunday on which Chance Wayne is castrated. The ruin of these religious holidays has its counterpart in the poor reception to Shannon's performance as a Christ figure in what Hannah calls a 'Passion Play' of his own. This time, however, the spoiled occasion is salutary. When Shannon finishes the intimate conversation with Hannah that follows, he has lived through the dark night of the soul and the writhing lizard in his flesh has been freed.

Although Hannah Jelkes, like Laura Wingfield, is one of Williams's never-blooming belles, she lives in neither the lost past nor the elusive future. The 'almost timeless quality' about Hannah to which Williams refers, or the Buddha-like tranquillity on which Shannon more than once remarks, comes from a beauty of soul, a spiritual dedication that by its nature is impervious to change. That is why, despite poverty, solitude and homelessness, she will lead hurt minds by still waters all her days, and hold fast to the eternal present.

The contrast between inside and outside in *Iguana* does not suggest the contest between creativity and destructive time that it does in *Menagerie* and *Streetcar*. The comings and goings on the hotel verandah mediate between the dim interior of the guest room where Nonno may be heard writing his poem, and the broad exterior defined by the rain forest and sea. Yet the inhabitants of the jungle are less to be feared than the cartoon-like German tank-manufacturer, who delights in hearing the news of the bombing of London on his portable radio as he and his family cross to and from the beach. The iguana, despite its appearance, is, at least in Hannah's view, 'one of God's creatures'. The ambiguous sea in which Shannon contemplates death and that Nonno calls 'the cradle of life' is like the 'Terra Incognita' in *Camino Real* that extends beyond the waystation of doubt and withdrawal. Shannon's reaching-out into the spectacular rainfall that ends the second act makes visual the position of man as a suppliant of nature's beneficence. The scenery of *Iguana*, with its cacti and flowering shrubbery, reminds us most of the lush and fruity setting of *The Rose Tattoo*. Indeed, a coconut tree arches over the verandah of the Costa Verde, bidding the weary traveller to take his ease, just as a palm tree leans dreamily over Serafina's cottage, inviting the reclusive widow to come out of doors.

The grace and serenity of the natural vegetation are continuous with that of the orange tree in Nonno's poem and finally with that of the heroine herself. When Hannah, just before Nonno dies, looks up and delivers the quiet curtain line, we are reminded of how the tree in the poem calmly observes the blanching sky:

And still the ripe fruit and the branch
Observe the sky begin to blanch
Without a cry, without a prayer,
With no betrayal of despair.

O Courage, could you not as well
Select a second place to dwell,

143

Not only in that golden tree
But in the frightened heart of me?

It is true that Hannah's line is a prayer to God for an end to human trial. Her heart is not quite so fearless as the tree. Yet no main character in a serious Williams play is more courageous. It is finally through Hannah's realisation of the wish contained in Nonno's last verse that Williams in *Iguana* reverses the outcome of his two personal myths.

The character of Jonathan Coffin is based on the Reverend Walter E. Dakin, grandfather of the playwright, who died in the year of *Cat on a Hot Tin Roof* (1955) at the age of ninety-eight. C. C., whose middle name was Coffin, died two years later. It was six years, therefore, before Williams, having closed out one phase of his career with a play that contains the death of the father, closed out another with one that shows the death of the grandfather. In each case the descendant is a sexually ambiguous figure in which the writer's twin masks may be seen to combine.

144

10
Late Plays (1962–81)

THE WRITER. They're disappearing behind me. Going.
People you've known in places do that: they go
when you go. The earth seems to swallow them up,
the walls absorb them like moisture, remain with
you only as ghosts; their voices are echoes, fading
but remembered.   (*Vieux Carré*)

In the two decades between *The Night of the Iguana* and
his death Williams wrote at least twenty-five more plays. In
them he continued to pursue his theme, loss in time,
although he never brought it to such a heartening
conclusion again. An increasing fear of age produces in his
late period a greater stridency of tone. His methods of work
– adaptation, expansion and recycling – underwent no
change. He persisted in the use of film techniques:
gratuitous music, 'plastic' lighting, ambiguous division
between interior and exterior. His structural model, the
modern short story, remained the same. In fact his
emphasis upon mood and character at the expense of plot

became even more pronounced. A few plays from the early and middle 1960s, such as *The Gnädiges Fräulein*, venture into the theatre of the absurd. Their black humour illustrates the new bitterness. Their anti-naturalism, however, is continuous with the willingness to experiment to be found in early one-act plays and short stories twenty years before them. Williams's more characteristic mode of lyric naturalism returns in the late 1960s and early 1970s with plays such as *Kingdom of Earth* and *Small Craft Warnings*. His final works, such as *Kirche, Kutchen, und Kinder* and *Something Cloudy, Something Clear*, gravitate toward the autobiographical material out of which his earliest had begun.

The transitional *Milk Train Doesn't Stop Here Anymore* (1964)[1] bridges the gap between the resolve of the naturalistic *Iguana* (1961) and the torment of the absurdist *The Gnädiges Fräulein* (1966). Two different versions of *Milk Train* were produced on Broadway in successive years. Herbert Machiz directed the 1963 production with Hermione Baddeley and Paul Roebling, Tony Robertson the 1964 production with Tallulah Bankhead and Tab Hunter. A film adaptation, *Boom!*, written by Williams and directed by Joseph Losey, was released in 1968, starring Richard Burton and Elizabeth Taylor. The play is a high-camp treatment of the encounter between the wanderer and the faded belle familiar from *Orpheus* and *Sweet Bird*. Christopher Flanders, a thirty-five-year-old itinerant poet and mobile sculptor whose name, like Val Xavier's, suggests salvation, has acquired the title of 'angel of death' by bringing sex and sympathy to rich, dying ladies on the Italian Riviera. He becomes the house guest of Sissie Goforth, a once beautiful but now aging ex-showgirl who makes it clear to him that she is no longer filled with the milk of human kindness. At the end, Sissie goes forth to die, and Chris, at least in the play's final version, survives. The ambiguity of *Milk Train* as a reversal play is in accord with the semi-abstract nature of its setting. Two stage assistants, dressed in black to establish their invisibility, move screens about and cue the actors, in accordance with the convention of the Kabuki Theatre.

The brittle comedy of *Milk Train* gives way to the black humour of *Slapstick Tragedy* (1966), the double bill under which *The Gnädiges Fräulein* and *The Mutilated* were first performed on Broadway in a production directed by Alan Schneider with Margaret Leighton in each of the two title roles. Both short plays present grotesque treatments of the faded belle. The *gnädiges Fräulein* ('gracious young lady') is an ex-singer and variety artist of genteel European background reduced in later years to competing with large carnivorous birds for her survival on the Florida keys. She had loved unrequitedly the Viennese dandy with whom she once performed before the crowned heads of Europe. Now half-crazed, she cherishes her scrapbook of old press clippings and makes pathetic efforts to sing on demand. At the end, having lost both eyes in her daily battle with the savage birds, she is bloodied but still unbowed. Williams called the 1974 expansion of the play *The Latter Days of a Celebrated Soubrette*. The central character of *The Mutilated* is Trinket Dugan, a once successful public relations woman from a wealthy Texan family. Now middle-aged and traumatised by mastectomy, she lives by herself in a run-down New Orleans hotel where her only companion at Christmas is Celeste Delacroix Griffin, a pugnacious, kleptomaniacal prostitute and freeloader whose equally serious mutilation is evident in the sorry spectacle of her discarded life.

The main set of both 'slapstick tragedies' is a transient residence whose dim interior suggests a fragile gentility in contrast with the sordidness and zany violence of the external world. Dressed in a pale rose kimono, Trinket sips tokay and plays the phonograph in her room at the head of the spindly staircase that rises outside the Silver Dollar Hotel while drunks, drifters, prostitutes and policemen appear on the street below. Similarly the Fräulein, dressed in the remnants of her theatrical wardrobe, lives in a cottage behind whose walls the suite of an old Viennese hotel seems to hide. The colourful display of crimson damask, gilt frame and potted ferns in the occasional light of the window is continuous with the 'splendours' of the Fräulein's past but at odds with what the landlady (Molly) describes to a local society editor (Polly) as 'a big dormitory' in which transients sleep on bunk beds. In any case, the once celebrated soubrette must now bring three fish back daily from the perilous docks in lieu of rent for each night's shelter.

Williams's archetypal actions, the eviction and the spoiled occasion, give thematic coherence to the brutal farces. Like her musical efforts, the Fräulein's plans to make an occasion of dinner are ruined. She cooks supper for the handsome primitive (Indian Joe) with whom she confuses her lost love, but the meal is stolen from the pan. As she stands on the porch at the end of the play, holding an empty skillet, Molly, Polly and Indian Joe sit at a 'festive' table within, preparing to enjoy the fish she gave her second eye to catch. Seconds later she races off to the docks again. But for the sightless heroine eviction now seems inevitable, unless the 'Dark Angel', who never leaves the cottage without company, chooses mercifully one morning to take her with him.

The pain of time's wounds stops only with death. In *The Mutilated* a figure in a black cowboy outfit (Jack in Black) appears among the carollers who intermittently sing of the comfort Christmas brings to the exiled, the maimed and the fugitive. It has brought little to Trinket and Celeste. Celeste is homeless; and, although Trinket can afford her room, shame has banished her from the world to which she rightly belongs. In this sense, she is also evicted just as Celeste is also mutilated. At the end the two women kneel before a vision of the Madonna in the belief that salvation is at hand. But Jack in Black is on holiday now; they will have to wait till he returns when Christmas is over.

Like the slapstick tragedies, the mid-length *Two-Character Play* (sometimes called *Out Cry*) belongs to Williams's experimental work of the 1960s. The version discussed here is that of the 1975 off-Broadway production. However, five different versions were staged over a period of nearly ten years, beginning with the 1967 London premiere directed by James Rosse-Evans with Mary Ure and Peter Wyngarde. Despite its Pirandellian form, *Two-Character* is a logical outgrowth of the one-act *I Can't Imagine Tomorrow* (1966), a strangely vague and intimate duologue that is itself anticipated by the earlier one-act *Talk to Me Like the Rain and Let Me Listen* (1953) and even by the closing exchanges of *The Lady of Larkspur Lotion* long before it.

In *Talk to Me* a man and a woman create out of their politeness and 'tender formality' a quiet place of refuge in the cruel city. This time he is the prostitute, as he is in *Orpheus, Sweet Bird* and *Milk Train*, 'passed around like a dirty post-card' from one night to the next. She is the literary one, who would live alone by the sea, communing only with the dead poets until, finally, when she is white with age, a wind – like the one Aunt Rose waits for in *Unsatisfactory Supper* – comes from somewhere beyond earth to bear her away. The nameless man and woman of *Talk to Me* foreshadow the equally anonymous One and

Two of *I Can't Imagine Tomorrow* as fugitive souls in hostile country whose only solace is one another. The blend of intimacy and anti-naturalistic vagueness in both duologues suggests a kind of reverie, as if the confessional playwright were engaged in a conversation with himself through what are plainly variations on his own twin masks.

The Two-Character Play is another of Williams's soliloquies in duologue form. The writing often consists of one character's completing a sentence begun by the other, just as it does in *I Can't Imagine*. The two characters are Felice and Clare Devoto, brother and sister, ostensibly the stars of a theatrical company that has deserted them during an international tour. On the stage of the state theatre in an unknown country, they attempt to perform, haltingly and with much resort to improvisation, what amounts to 'a play in progress' about the trauma of their lives. The indifferent audience soon walks out. When at the end they discover that they are locked within an empty, cold and darkening house, they resume their performance in the vain attempt to conclude it by mutual suicide.

Felice has the look of a deranged poet in his ankle-length coat and his shoulder-length hair. Indeed, he is a writer as well as a performer. The neurasthenic and vaguely spectral Clare, with her streaked blonde hair and broken tiara, alternates between haughtiness and vulgarity when she is not being solemnly childlike. Both appear youthful without being young. Fragments of scenery from different plays – including a throne-sized chair and a papier-mâché giant – clutter the vast, dimly lit backstage area, creating a jumble of 'dismaying shapes and shadows' that suggests not only a collapsed intellect but also the phantasmagoric world in which 'we all of us live at present'. At the centre, the set for the play-within-the-play represents the Victorian living-room of a house in summer, deep in the American South.

Felice and Clare are the son and daughter of a frigid mother and a wild-spirited father who earned a living by giving astrological readings. The father shot his wife and then himself when she threatened to commit him to the state asylum. Owing to the manner of his death, the orphaned children received no benefits from their father's life insurance. They became recluses, afraid to leave the house even to buy food. The neighbours believed them to be crazed.

Whether Clare and Felice are actors playing themselves or asylum inmates playing actors playing themselves, the play and the play-within-the-play work together in complementary fashion to show the brother and the sister locked within an unbreakable circle of dread and pain. 'The house has turned to a prison', says Felice. 'I've always suspected that theatres are prisons for players', says Clare. The papier-mâché giant of the outer play corresponds to the giant sunflower of the inner play that, Felice tells Clare, now stands taller than the house. The two characters are grown-up children in Beanstalk Country. Their development having been arrested by their terrible loss, they must continue to re-enact the experience of it for as long as they live, even if it means doing so before an empty house in a city unknown.

The resemblance of Felice and Clare, respectively, to the wanderer and the faded belle reminds us of the earlier appearance of Williams's twin archetypes as the brother and sister in *The Glass Menagerie*, a play with which *Two-Character* shares the idea of enacting in the form of a play-within-a-play the memory of a haunting and inescapable past. The ironically named Felice (Happy) and Clare (Bright) allude directly to Tom and Rose Williams during their late childhood in St Louis as reclusive intimates at odds with an alien environment. Just as the

Williams children were snubbed for being Southerners, the Devoto orphans are taunted for being 'loonies'. Insults and obscenities come to them through the mail, accusations appear in the paper, and a neighbour's child continually pellets their house with his slingshot.

The threat of eviction or homelessness is a primary condition of both the inner play and the outer play, helping to bind the two into a single dramatic unit. Before the 'performance' Felice tells Clare that the theatre is their home. But it is a scenic replication of the house they grew up in to which the actors habitually repair. They even take off their coats when they resume their performance toward the end, because they are stepping from the actual cold of the theatre into the imaginary heat of a Southern summer. Only such warmth, comfort and seclusion as they are able to create by artistic effort are available to Clare and Felice. Yet that effort is dedicated to the enactment of the loss of those very things. 'Confinement', we learn, is their 'prohibited word'. Paradoxically, what they are 'confined' to is the permanent dread of homelessness.

There is a darkening of the tone in Williams's late period that this grim and humourless play serves to illustrate. A character's presentation of his life story to a poor critical reception is a version of the spoiled occasion that frequently occurs among the early one-act plays. The poignancy of this archetypal action in *Portrait of a Madonna* and *Lord Byron's Love Letter*, however, is in *Two-Character* displaced by the new bitterness. The trauma of disappointment in love gives way to that of parental death. Flight and reclusiveness turn into agoraphobia. Time stopped for Felice and Clare when their mother and father died, just as it did for Lucretia Collins when the man she loved married another or for Irénée de Poitevent when her enchanted summer came to an end. But nostalgia for the lost past is only a faint glimmer in *Two-Character*, a few lines about a holiday at the beach before the children were old enough for school. The dominant note is an outcry of anguish from a deepening well of pain.

Williams reverted to his more naturalistic manner with *Kingdom of Earth*, called *The Seven Descents of Myrtle* in the first (1968) Broadway production directed by José Quintero, with Harry Guardino as Chicken, Estelle Parsons as Myrtle, and Brian Bedford as Lot. The 1970 screen adaptation, called *Last of the Mobile Hot Shots* in the United States and *Blood Kin* abroad, was written by Gore Vidal and directed by Sidney Lumet, with Lynn Redgrave as Myrtle, James Coburn as Jeb, and Robert Hooks as Chicken. The scene is a poor Mississippi Delta farmhouse through whose transparent rear wall we may enter, like a film camera, to observe a kitchen, a hallway, a staircase, an upstairs bedroom, and a mysterious little 'parlour' with a crystal chandelier and golden chairs. This last is the familiar 'poetic' interior, the lost place of refuge or gentility.

Kingdom of Earth is a three-character play based on a one-act (1967) that derives from an earlier short story (1954).[2] The characters are a young, fatally ill transvestite (Lot Ravenstock), his wife of two days (Myrtle), and his animalistic half-brother (Chicken). In the action, set against a background of rising flood waters, Chicken survives Lot to inherit his wife and his land. The triangle is reminiscent of *Streetcar*, in which the widow of the dead homosexual is possessed carnally by her ape-like brother-in-law. Lot is not yet dead before Chicken breaks through Myrtle's feeble protestations just as Stanley cruelly degrades Blanche. In *Kingdom of Earth*, however, the faded belle is less the malleable wife (an ex-showgirl) than she is the 'exotically pretty' husband, who, with his pale eyes and dyed blond hair, dresses up like a ghost of his mother in her youth and dies in her beloved parlour.

The fall of a sensitive creature and the rise of his tougher counterpart is the action in common between *Kingdom of Earth* and *In the Bar of a Tokyo Hotel*, a mid-length play which received its world premiere in the off-Broadway production of 1969 directed by Herbert Machiz with Ann Meacham as Miriam and Donald Madden as Mark. The sickly Lot Ravenstock corresponds to the psychotic Mark Conley, a painter whose inability to control his new technique has driven him into a state of infantile dependency. When he dies in torment in a Japanese hotel, his predatory wife (Miriam) is at last free of him. The pathetic death of the failed painter reverses the heroic death of the victorious writer, D. H. Lawrence, in the early one-act *I Rise in Flame, Cried the Pheonix* (written *c*. 1941). Lawrence, whose role in history as a sexual rebel made him one of Williams's first literary idols, commands his wife (Frieda) to stand clear of him when the time comes. That the Conleys, unlike the Lawrences, are bound in a symbiotic relationship helps to explain why the dialogue of *Tokyo Hotel* continues the experiment in truncated lines that started with *I Can't Imagine* and *Two-Character*. A word is as good as a phrase in a conversation between intimates. Miriam asks Mark whether they are two people or only one. The answer is that they are two sides of Tennessee Williams, torn between defeat and defiance as responses to failure in age.

The only popular success that Williams enjoyed after *Iguana* was *Small Craft Warnings*, a mid-length play first presented in the 1972 off-Broadway production directed by Richard Altman with Helena Carroll as Leona. To boost sales, the playwright himself sometimes appeared in the role of Doc. In *Small Craft Warnings* Williams once more returned to his familiar mode of lyric naturalism. The work bears some resemblance to Saroyan's *Time of Your Life* and even to O'Neill's *Iceman Cometh* in that the action takes place in a bar to which the customers, all losers in life, come regularly to spend their time and tell their stories. In *Small Craft* it is a bar on the California coast, or rather the 'nonrealistic evocation' of one. All three walls give the effect of fog rolling in from the sea. The uncertain division between interior and exterior is a film convention, like the mood music of the convenient juke box that plays under the big speeches while on the darkened set a spot picks out the actor to create the equivalent of a close-up. In the one-act *Confessional* (1970), of which *Small Craft* is an expansion, each customer (and even the barman himself) delivers his key speech to the house from a special area downstage of the bar called the 'confessional'. The 'confession' is essentially the individual's 'story', the familiar self-revelation of Williams's stage people that ordinarily encounters a poor reception. Since in this case only the audience is privy to it, the confession reduces plot by defining character in the absence of dramatic interaction. *Small Craft* compromises with naturalism by moving the soliloquies from the abstract area down stage into the bar itself. The structural principle, however, remains what it is in the one-act play: a collection of character sketches or short stories.

What binds them together are the common conditions of loss, solitude and inconsequence. A lachrymose nymphomaniac (Violet) lives (it is 'a temporary arrangement') in a room without a toilet over an amusement arcade. A homosexual screenwriter (Quentin) has been so deadened by the coarse and ephemeral nature of his relationships that he has lost the ability to be surprised. A physician (Doc) who has lost his licence for operating while drunk must turn fugitive after an illegal delivery in which neither mother nor child survived.

The apparent exception within this sorry group is the central character (Leona Dawson), a large, boisterous woman in her late thirties dressed in a pair of white clamdigger's slacks, a pink sweater and a sailor's hat over her dyed corkscrew curls. She lives in a trailer and earns her living as an itinerant beautician. The action occurs on the anniversary of the death of her brother, a handsome young homosexual violinist whom she adored. The theme music is 'Souvenir', a violin piece that Leona repeatedly plays on the bar's juke box. Thus the position in *Glass Menagerie* of the seafaring brother's remembering his sister is here reversed. For that matter, Leona's courageous willingness to endure begins to ally her with Hannah Jelkes as an inversion of the defeated wanderer. She honours her brother's memory and is outraged by the shabby treatment she has received from her present lover, but she will not be subdued. She has always affirmed life in the past and vows that she will continue to do so in the future.

Nevertheless, the maudlin and strident notes that enter Williams's work after *Iguana* dominate *Small Craft Warnings*. Leona is surrounded by others whose adjustment to pain and change ranges from whimpering dependency to total jadedness. Even she admits that her many heartbreaks will never mend and that her dead brother (Haley), who played the violin in church and was cut down by pernicious anaemia in his youth, is the one beautiful thing she has to look back on. The mounted sailfish over the bar contrasts with the fragile souls that circle below it, some adrift, some struggling, and others already shipwrecked on the lonely, troubled sea of life in time.

In the mid-1970s Williams continued to project his

sense of loss and decay through varieties of the faded belle. In *The Red Devil Battery Sign* she appears as a half-crazed, rebellious aristocrat (Woman Downtown) reminiscent of Carol Cutrere in *Orpheus Descending*, a state senator's daughter who leaves her wealthy husband for a fatally ill musician, and upon the death of her lover becomes the consort of an adolescent gang-leader. In *This Is: An Entertainment*, a fantastic farce set in a time of revolution, she appears in inverted form as an ex-prostitute turned countess whose outrageous narcissism reminds us of Sissie Goforth in *Milk Train* and Miriam Conley in *Tokyo Bar*. Her uncompromising dedication to the sensual experience of the living 'mo-ment' mocks the elegiac author's own inclination to dwell in the dead past. She offers herself to the successful revolutionary general after her husband jumps out the window with an umbrella for a parachute. The first production of *Red Devil*, directed by Edwin Sherin with Anthony Quinn as King Del Rey and Claire Bloom as the Woman Downtown, closed in Boston in 1975. A revised version opened in London two years later. *This Is* received its world premiere in San Francisco in 1976 in a production directed by Allen Fletcher with Elizabeth Huddle as the Countess and Ray Reinhardt as the Count. Both these sprawling spectacles reflect the upheaval in American society during the Vietnam period, as does the one-act *Demolition Downtown* (1971), whose two middle-class housewives, like the Countess, plan to offer themselves to the leaders of a rebellion. The one-act play also shares with *This Is* the truncated sentences and brittle comedy that were first combined in *Tokyo Hotel*.

Both the wanderer and the faded belle appear in *Vieux Carré*,[3] an episodic play based on Williams's reminiscences of his life in a shabby New Orleans rooming-house during 1938–9. The original Broadway production was directed by

Arthur Allan Seidelman in 1977 with Sylvia Sidney as Mrs Wire and Richard Alfieri as the Writer. The work incorporates the early short story 'Angel in the Alcove', in which Williams recalls seeing a ghostly figure resembling his maternal grandmother by the window of his room. In *Vieux Carré* the wanderer is the young Williams himself (the Writer), who, like Tom Wingfield in *Menagerie*, serves as both narrator and participant. There is a tubercular painter (Nightingale) with whom the Writer has a homosexual relationship, a black servant (Nursie) who is long past the age of retirement, and two pathetic old ladies (Miss Carrie and Mary Maude) who have been reduced to picking their food out of the garbage. The faded belle is a Northern variant of the fallen Southern gentlewoman, a might-have-been fashion-illustrator of genteel background from upstate New York (Jane Sparks) who, now fatally stricken with tuberculosis, shares a room with a Kowalski-like strip show barker (Tye McCool). Her ladylike demeanour and slightly dated eloquence remind us most of Mrs Hardwicke-Moore in *The Lady of Larkspur Lotion*. Her complaint to the landlady (Mrs Wire) about the flying cockroaches in her room is only a minor revision of the former heroine's speech on the same topic to the landlady of the same name in the early one-act play. The hard-headed Mrs Wire of *Larkspur Lotion*, however, becomes a sympathetic role in *Vieux Carré*, a major character who herself partakes of the loneliness and mental instability of the faded belle.

At the end of the play, the dying Jane has dismissed her lover, the dying Nightingale has been taken to the hospital, and the Writer has gone west with a young vagrant as did Williams himself. Such unity as this kaleidoscopic drama enjoys is primarily owing to its sense of place. In the courtyard below the guest rooms tourists may be heard admiring the faded elegance of the old mansion, humbled by time and transformed in the imagination of the nostalgic author into a metaphor of life's melancholy transience. In his opening stage directions Williams calls for 'a poetic evocation of all the cheap rooming houses of the world'. The fleeting events that occur within its shadows comprise an elegiac vision of deaths and departures.

The faded belle reappears in *A Lovely Sunday for Creve Coeur*[4] as a neurasthenic, 'marginally youthful' schoolteacher from Memphis (Dorothea Gallaway) now living in a drab St Louis apartment during the Depression. The play was presented off Broadway in 1979 in a production directed by Keith Hack with Shirley Knight as Dorothea and Peg Murray as Bodey. An earlier version had been produced in Charleston, South Carolina, the previous year. Dorothea, like Blanche DuBois and Alma Winemiller, having invalidated in the past the sexuality of the man she idealised, is punished in the present by the man to whom she succumbs. In her youth she had rejected a young musician she greatly admired who suffered from what a doctor told her was an incurable sexual affliction. In the play she waits all morning for a telephone call from the philandering high-school principal she expects to marry only to read in the paper that he is engaged to someone else. The question is what will happen to her in the future. The three other women in the play suggest the alternatives. Her colleague (Helena Brookmire) is a cynical spinster. Her neighbour (Sophie Gluck) is a helpless psychotic. Her flatmate (Bodey) is a dumpy, family-minded woman of German descent with a twin brother (Buddy) who wants to get married. Whether or not Dorothea is quite ready to accept him, she ends the play by leaving to meet the twins for a picnic in the well-named park (Creve Coeur). Perhaps, like Leona Dawson of *Small Craft*, she will decide to make the best of things; as she leaves, she tells Sophie one must go on. But settling for drab domesticity after great expectations serves only to underscore the playwright's familiar action of loss and decline.

The disturbing history of Zelda Fitzgerald, central character of *Clothes for a Summer Hotel*,[5] represents a more precipitous fall. The literary, sophisticated, once-beautiful Montgomery belle is finally burned alive in her last asylum after her deep disappointment in a marriage whose public appearance was the stuff of legend. *Clothes* received its world premiere in 1980 in the Broadway production directed by José Quintero, with Geraldine Page as Zelda and Kenneth Haigh as Scott. The play hints at Zelda's unsatisfied sensuality by contrasting Scott's vaguely feminine looks with the heroic presence of the French aviator with whom she has a brief affair. Zelda, years later, practises her bar exercises in the asylum with the pathetic hope of realising her early ambition to become a dancer. The influence of the expressionist Strindberg, obvious in Williams's dream play, *Camino Real*, is also evident in the 'ghost play'. Its spectral evocation of the Fitzgeralds and of the jazz age whose excitement they embodied comes with the sad realisation that we are witness to the mere shadows of the famous couple, whose lives, for all their youthful glamour, ended in alcoholism, heart failure, insanity and immolation.

Clothes was the last Broadway premiere of a Williams play before the author's death in 1983 and is his last published full-length play to date. A posthumous edition of four unproduced scripts for film or television appeared in 1984,[6] but they were all written ten to thirty years beforehand. With the exception of *One Arm* (*c*. 1972), an adaptation of the early short story, they focus on a version of the faded belle. In *Stopped Rocking* (*c*. 1975) a female mental patient suffers a complete withdrawal when her husband tells her he plans to remarry. In *The Loss of a Teardrop Diamond* (*c*. 1955) a highly strung Southern debutante purchases the favours of a handsome but needy young man. *All Gaul is Divided* (*c*. 1958) is a film treatment of *Creve Coeur* that Williams says he forgot when he came to write the play in the 1970s. Some of the one-act plays in *Theatre*, vols vi–vii (1981), appear in print for the first time, but they are not all late works. *Steps Must Be Gentle*, a brief duologue between the ghosts of Hart Crane and his mother, was written in the year of *Streetcar* (1947). The epigraphs for *Streetcar* and *Sweet Bird* are both quotations from the young homosexual poet, who, like one of Williams's wanderers, committed suicide by drowning at sea. *Now the Cats with Jewelled Claws*, a libretto for opera and dance, dates from 1969, when it was titled *Now and at the Hour of Our Death*. It is a bitter comedy in which two narcissistic women are contrasted with two doomed homosexual prostitutes, of whom one dies and the other is given a glimpse of his humiliating future.

Williams's last one-act plays, most of them written with the savage self-mockery of the slapstick tragedies, reflect his desperate fear of helplessness in old age. *This is the Peaceable Kingdom* or *Good Luck God* is a sad and terrifying work set in a poor New York nursing-home during the strike of 1978. The alternate title quotes the ironic graffito on the wall before which the enfeebled and incontinent patients sit in their wheelchairs. *Peaceable Kingdom* pursues the subject of the earlier *Frosted Glass Coffin* (1970), an equally grim play set in a low-priced Miami retirement hotel whose residents, boxed in by their aged bodies, can only see what life remains to them through tear-strained, cataract-blinded eyes. *Lifeboat Drill* is a farce in which a wealthy nonagenarian couple, suffering from every geriatric affliction, struggle to put on life-preservers in their first-class cabin in the QE2 for the mandatory shipboard drill. Finally, *The Travelling Companion*[7] is a brief duologue in a New York hotel room between one who is plainly the lonely, ailing author himself (Vieux) and a young homosexual prostitute (Beaux) whom he has employed.

The unpublished full-length plays of 1980–1 were produced off Broadway or out of town. A semi-professional production of *Will Mr Merriwether Return from Memphis?* marked the opening of the Tennessee Williams Fine Arts Center at Florida Keys Community College in 1980. *Merriwether* is a faded-belle reversal play written more than a decade earlier, a romantic fantasy, in the style of *Camino Real*, whose lovelorn, middle-aged heroine (Louise McBride) finds happiness at last upon the miraculous return of the travelling salesman (Mr Merriwether), who had once, long ago, been a boarder in her home. In 1981 *A House not Meant to Stand* received its premiere at the Goodman Theatre, Chicago. Derived from the earlier one-act *Some Problems for the Moose Lodge, House* is what Williams calls 'a Gothic Comedy' about a Mississippi family, a painfully nostalgic work, larded with country humour, that reminds us most of *Cat*. It contains a blustering, money-grubbing father (Cornelius McCorkle), his half-crazed, persevering wife (Bella) and their three children: a psychotic daughter (Joanie), a heterosexual son engaged to be married (Charlie), and a homosexual son recently deceased (Chips). At the end Bella dies and Charlie inherits her money. The play is of interest to students of Williams as the second of two in the canon to present a character based on the playwright's brother, Dakin (he appears first as Gooper in *Cat*). An early stage direction asserts that the McCorkle home is 'a metaphor for the state of society'. Whether or not the work quite succeeds as a prediction of social downfall, it leaves no doubt that from the viewpoint of the confessional author the house of Williams was not meant to stand.

Two equally autobiographical plays were produced by Jean Cocteau Repertory, an off-off-Broadway group well suited to Williams's 'plastic' or cinematic stagecraft because dedicated to what Cocteau called 'a poetry of the theatre' (opposed to one *in* the theatre): that is, not verse drama, but a symbolic use of non-verbal elements within a theatrical whole. In the Cocteau's production of *Kirche, Kutchen, und Kinder* (1980) time was told only by the daisy of day that unfolded against the upstage wall or the night-blooming vine that as slowly crawled down it. Labelled 'an Outrage for the Stage' in the programme, *Kirche, Kutchen, und Kinder* is an outlandish comic strip based on the author's experience of life in his sixties. The central figure is a retired male prostitute (the Man) in tight pants, T-shirt and studded belt who, although he can still manage to do somersaults, pretends to be confined to a wheelchair. He is writing his memoirs (Williams had published his own in 1975) in the *Kirche*, a secluded room into which a veiled young woman (Miss Rose) periodically enters to accompany his soliloquies on the organ. His wife (the Woman) is a pert but frumpy *Hausfrau* who spends most of her time in the *Kutchen* (the error in the old phrase defining woman's role is consistent with the Katzenjammer German she speaks). Their *Kinder* are an adolescent boy and girl in children's clothing who, having failed kindergarten, are being taught by their father to become prostitutes. The Woman's father (the Lutheran Minister) is an abnormally tall figure (elevated by cothurni) in a stovepipe hat and a black swallow-tailed coat. He carries an outsize Bible and an umbrella with which he frequently knocks his daughter over the head. In the performance, each time he did so she reeled from the blow, cross-eyed, and birds chirped in the air. The scenes alternate between the slapstick encounters in the *Kutchen* and the hero's long speeches in the *Kirche* during which he jokes with the audience, explains character and set, reminisces, and comments dreamily on life, time, and beauty. He insists that he is above all a survivor. At the end, disappointed by the *Kinder*'s having given themselves away for love instead of holding out for money, he stands up from his chair to everyone's surprise, buckles on his studded belt, and announces his decision to return to work within the zany, violent world from which he has only pretended to have been forced to retire.

The gaudy colours of *Kirche, Kutchen, und Kinder* faded to the pastel shades of *Something Cloudy, Something Clear* (1981), a memory play in the vein of *Menagerie* and *Vieux Carré*. This time the Williams character appeared as a thirty-year-old writer in khaki trousers and unbuttoned shirt (August) who, while revising a play in Provincetown over the summer of 1940, meets a needy young man and woman, both fatally ill (Kip and Claire), with whom he plans to live later on in the autumn. All that actually happens is that he completes his revisions and initiates Kip into homosexuality. In the course of the play he receives a visit from his producer (Maurice Fiddler), who agrees to his terms, and another from a noted actress (Caroline Wales), who expresses her enthusiasm for the main female role. In her scene Caroline recites a speech from *Battle of Angels*, a play whose Theatre Guild production failed in Boston at the end of 1940. If she is a mask for its star, Miriam Hopkins, then Maurice Fiddler is one for the Guild's founder, Lawrence Langner, Kip is one for a young man of that name Williams knew in Provincetown that summer, and Claire is one for the young woman Kip married after a brief homosexual experience with Williams. It was in late August 1940 that the author, according to his *Memoirs*, left Provincetown for Mexico after Kip severed their relationship. Eight years later Williams dedicated his first volume of stories to Kip, who died of brain cancer in his twenties.

Complementing the visitors to August's lonely shack in the dunes, voices from his past and his future seem to address him from the sky. The dying Frank Merlo echoes the doomed Kip, the soothing Hazel Kramer the compassionate Claire, and even the outspoken Tallulah Bankhead, who turned down the lead in *Battle*, the grateful Caroline Wales, who accepts it. August's comment (it was quoted in the Cocteau programme) best summarises the point of these associations: 'Life is all – it's just one time, it finally seems to occur at one time'. The play's title alludes to the mingling of past and future in a montage of present images, clear and cloudy. It also refers to the elegiac drama of Tennessee Williams. Under August's line the programme quoted Rilke's ninth Sonnet to Orpheus, which closes with the thought that it is only in the 'double-world', the blurry reflection in a pool of water, that 'voices become eternal and mild'. The Cocteau's *Something Cloudy* ended with Kip and Claire dancing in slow motion while August, standing in the light upstage, told us how he remembered them from that summer half a lifetime ago. Like the mythical poet and singer with whom he so often identified, the playwright had descended into the realm of the dead once more, and returned to create from their clear and cloudy forms the double world of his art, in which the troubled and transient experience of life in time is transformed into that which is eternal and mild.

Conclusion

CASSANDRA WHITESIDE. That's the graveyard, honey.
It's situated, appropriately enough, on the highest
point of land in Two River County, a beautiful
windy bluff just west of the Sunflower
River. (*Battle of Angels*)

The centre of Williams's mythological world is a place
within the Mississippi Delta called Two River County.
Analogous to Faulkner's Yoknapatawpha, it provides the
setting, or at least the background, for the playwright's
most characteristic work. Two River County, with its towns
of Lyon, Sunset, Blue Mountain and Glorious Hill, its
Moon Lake and Moon Lake Casino, its Reverend Tooker
and Drs Buchanan, is a phantasmagoric landscape of
deaths and longings in which fatal shootings occur, illness
takes its toll, fires rage in the darkness, and black flood
waters push into oblivion the fragile dreams of the past.
Death and desire mingle at Moon Lake, seen nearly always

at night, by whose shore the wine orchard of Lady Torrance's father was once a haven for drinking and love-making until burned down by the Mystic Crew with the old Italian in it who made the mistake of serving blacks. Moon Lake Casino in the first years of the century, operated by the pistol-carrying Papa Gonzales, is a dangerous attraction for drinking, gambling and easy sex, where Alma Winemiller will not watch the illegal spectacle of cock fighting and John Buchanan receives a knife wound in a brawl. It is at the edge of Moon Lake that Allan Grey shoots himself after leaving the dance floor of the casino, where minutes earlier his young wife, Blanche, told him that she disgusted her. One of Amanda Wingfield's beaux dies in a shooting duel at the casino, and another drowns in the lake. Val Xavier is lynched in Two River County. We know that it will also be the place of Big Daddy Pollitt's death, because it is on the track of the Glorious Hill High School that Brick fractures an ankle the night before his father's terrible birthday. The Reverend Tooker, who appears in *Cat*, is mentioned in *Orpheus* as the Episcopal minister of Vee Talbott's church, a one-time Methodist who had preached against Lady Torrance's father during Prohibition days. Moreover, the terminally ill Jabe Torrance of *Orpheus* is a patient of the unseen elder Dr Buchanan, and even the younger is referred to by his nickname, Dr Johnny, although his father dies of a gunshot wound in *Summer and Smoke*, a play set in a time fifty years earlier. Like the fabled Pollitt plantation, the territory of the legendary Delta drummer, Charlie Colton, extends into Two River County, where only yesterday in the lounge of the Elks Club at Blue Mountain yet another old friend has died. Alva, sister of the thirteen-year-old Willie of *This Property is Condemned*, succumbs to tuberculosis in Two River County or very near it, as does the pitiable Lot

Ravenstock, and the rivers, having broken their banks, cover over his lost kingdom of earth.

The region is a vision of an Eden gone to seed, a fallen world with memories of paradise. Its Glorious Hill, a town whose name commemorates past triumph, is on the route of Lady Torrance's calliope as it rolls through the county to announce the intended opening of her doomed confectionary. The father of the pathetic 'madonna', Lucretia Collins, once preached in Glorious Hill; the Nightingale of the Delta, Alma Winemiller, used to sing there; and the handsome Brick Pollitt left it, crowned with early laurels, to return an alcoholic under thirty. At neighbouring Blue Mountain, home of the young Amanda Wingfield, who entertained seventeen gentleman callers one afternoon, the infantile Flora Meighan is raped by the Syndicate superintendent, and the aging Aunt Rose endures her final eviction. Uncle Pleasant, wild spirit in a land sick with neon, also comes from Blue Mountain, while not far off, an easy drive from Moon Lake, the old plantation house of Belle Reve still stands, fond dream of an age gone by.

Two River County is a metaphorical assertion of Williams's elegiac sensibility. Its grim view of the postbellum South contributes less to history than it does to the agrarian myth. The real Moon Lake, four miles long and shaped like a crescent moon, is eighteen miles from Clarksdale in Coahoma County in the northwest corner of Mississippi. There is no casino. Blue Mountain is a small town of less than a thousand in Tippah County in the northeast corner of the state and a long way from the Delta. There is no Glorious Hill. Clarksdale, however, a city built on the confluence of the Big and Little Sunflower Rivers, was the Williams home for the last three years in Mississippi (1915–18) before the family moved to St Louis.

Conclusion

Since Williams felt that the end of early childhood in the deep South was like the loss of paradise, it is likely that the inspiration for the two rivers of his mythological county was not only the Big and Little Sunflower but also the Tigris and Euphrates, which framed the ancient land known in Greek as 'between rivers' or Mesopotamia, and at the source of which the first Eden was said to be situated. In any case, it is clear that Two River County, once blessed, is now forsaken, a symbolic landscape where lost souls, like the first fugitives from paradise, endure their dark odyssey through time.

The winds of death and transience blow across Two River County and beyond it to New Orleans and the Gulf. They are in Mexico and California, in St Louis and New York, wherever a Williams play is set. They are the sighing in the palms that merges with the thematic music of *Sweet Bird*. They are the sorrowful murmur from the deep blue dusk the evening Jim O'Connor calls in *Menagerie*. They are the loud singing heard against the measured reverberations of the surf in the remote locales of *Milk Train* and *Camino*. They are in the ghost plays, *Steps Must Be Gentle* and *Clothes*, moving the heavy seas that separate Hart Crane from his mother and bringing the scudding drifts at sunset over the hill where Zelda Fitzgerald died by fire in her last asylum. They signal the pitying rain that falls after the suicides in *The Purification* and sweep clean the silent sky to which Hannah Jelkes appeals at the end of *Iguana* the moment before her grandfather dies in his chair. It is a rare Williams work, early or late, in which the movement toward dissolution is not prominent. The death of the defiant D. H. Lawrence, writer and painter, of the early *I Rise in Flame*, is matched by the death of the defeated Mark Conley, painter, of the late *Tokyo Hotel*. Among the first plays, the ruined Bertha writes a brief hello to the man who broke her heart and the nostalgic Joe Bassett a long goodbye to his childhood. Irénée de Poitevent has no life but the one she finished in early youth, and Eloi Duvenet ends his own by fire. Among the last plays, *The Red Devil Battery Sign* and *This Is: An Entertainment* contemplate the return to barbarism in the wake of social upheaval. *Something Cloudy, Something Clear* and *Vieux Carré* are journeys to the ghostly past. *Life-Boat Drill, The Frosted Glass Coffin*, and *This is the Peaceable Kingdom* focus, respectively, on old age, degenerative illness and impending death.

A lament for losses never to be restored courses through Williams's drama. Sometimes it is cut off by the tourniquet of comedy. Sometimes it flows freely, creating a pool of bittersweet nostalgia. Sometimes it rises in a flood of heated rage. Sometimes it is channelled in thin streams over surfaces pre-empted by prior concerns. But it is always there – in the homesickness, in the death of poets, in the lovelorn women and the lonely men, in the sweet memories of an enchanted age long ago, in the transience of beauty, the corruption of innocence, the futility of art and, finally, in the disappointed ideal of a divine order of being. For, after all, the wanderer and the faded belle are both wayward souls in the purgatory of time. The plunge to ruin of Blanche DuBois from the high columns of Belle Reve is an image of a second fall of man, like the coming down to earth of Chance Wayne from St Cloud or of Val Xavier to the Underworld from the fields of Heavenly Grass.

Notes

1. Introduction and Life

1. The following essays, cited in this chapter, can most easily be found in *Where I Live* (New York: New Directions, 1978): 'Facts About Me' (1952), 'On a Streetcar Named Success' (1947), 'Something Wild' (1945).
2. Included in *Hard Candy* (New York: New Directions, 1954).

2. Form, Theme and Character

1. George Brandt, 'Cinematic Structure in the Work of Tennessee Williams', in *American Theatre*, ed. J. R. Brown and B. Harris (London: Edward Arnold, 1967) p. 168.
2. W. R. Mueller, 'Tennessee Williams: A New Direction?', *Christian Century*, LXXXI (14 Oct 1964) 1271.

3. Early One-Act Plays

1. *Moony's Kid Don't Cry, The Dark Room, Ten Blocks on the Camino Real*, and *The Case of the Crushed Petunias* are most easily found in *American Blues* (New York: Dramatists Play Service, 1948). Unless otherwise noted, all the other short plays discussed in this chapter are in *Theatre*, VI.
2. Williams probably mistook Irénée, a male saint's name, for the

French form of Irene. The playwright's use of foreign words and names is not always accurate.

3. In *American Scenes*, ed. William Kozlenko (New York: John Day, 1941).

4. Ibid. *Property* was the starting-point for a 1966 film of the same name written by Francis Ford Coppola *et al.* and directed by Sidney Pollack with Natalie Wood and Robert Redford.

5. Williams pays homage to his father in one of his last short stories, 'The Man in the Overstuffed Chair', *Antaeus*, 45–6 (Spring–Summer 1982) 281–92.

6. Bellerive is a small town ten miles west of St Louis. In the film of *Streetcar*, as in the play's original production, Belle Reve is pronounced as if it were spelled 'Bellereeve'.

4.   'The Glass Menagerie'

1. For an excellent demonstration of this point, see Judith Thompson, 'Symbol, Myth, and Ritual in *The Glass Menagerie, The Rose Tattoo*, and *Orpheus Descending*', in *Tennessee Williams: A Tribute*, ed. Jac Tharpe (Jackson: University Press of Mississippi, 1977) pp. 697–711.

2. The cited reviews of the 1945 premiere production of *The Glass Menagerie* are: Robert Garland, in *New York Journal-American*, 2 Apr 1945, repr. in *New York Theatre Critics' Reviews, 1945*, p. 235; Wolcott Gibbs, in *New Yorker*, 21 (7 Apr 1945) 40; Stark Young, in *New Republic*, 112 (16 Apr 1945) 505–6; Joseph Wood Krutch, in *Nation*, 160 (14 Apr 1945) 424–5.

3. For the 1956 production, see Walter Kerr, in *New York Herald-Tribune*, 22 Nov 1956, repr. in *New York Theatre Critics' Reviews, 1956*, p. 190. For the 1965 production, see Richard Watts, Jr, in *New York Post*, 5 May 1965, repr. in *New York Theatre Critics' Reviews, 1965*, p. 332.

4. Thomas L. King, 'Irony and Distance in *The Glass Menagerie*', *Educational Theatre Journal*, xxv, no. 2 (May 1973) 207–14.

5. The cited reviews of the 1975 New York production of *The Glass Menagerie* are: Clive Barnes, in *New York Times*, 19 Dec 1975, and Douglas Watt, in *New York Daily News*, 19 Dec 1975, repr. in *New York Theatre Critics' Reviews, 1975*, pp. 125 and 128; T. E. Kalem, in *Time*, 107 (12 Jan 1976) 61.

5.   'A Streetcar Named Desire'

1. This motive is explicit in some early drafts of the play. See Vivienne Dickson, '*A Streetcar Named Desire*: Its Development through the Manuscripts', in *Tennessee Williams: A Tribute*, ed. Tharpe, pp. 154–71.

Notes

2. For details of the physical production, see Robert Downing, 'Streetcar Conductor: Some Notes from Backstage', *Theatre Annual*, 8 (1950) 25–33.

3. The cited reviews of *A Streetcar Named Desire* are: William Hawkins, in *New York World-Telegram*, 4 Dec 1947; Howard Barnes, in *New York Herald-Tribune*, 4 Dec 1947; Robert Coleman, in *New York Daily Mirror*, 4 Dec 1947; and Brooks Atkinson, in *New York Times*, 4 Dec 1947: all repr. in *New York Theatre Critics' Reviews, 1947*, pp. 251–2. Also cited: John Mason Brown, in *Saturday Review*, 30 (27 Dec 1947) 22–4; Harold Clurman, 'Tennessee Williams' (1948), *Lies Like Truth* (New York: Macmillan, 1958) pp. 72–80; Eric Bentley, 'Better Than Europe?' (1949), *In Search of Theatre* (New York: Atheneum, 1975) pp. 87–9.

4. See Elia Kazan, 'Notebook for *A Streetcar Named Desire*', in *Directors on Directing*, ed. Toby Cole and Helen C. Chinoy rev. edn (Indianapolis: Bobbs Merrill, 1963) pp. 364–73.

6. 'Summer and Smoke'

1. The cited reviews of *Summer and Smoke* are: Brooks Atkinson, in *New York Times*, 7 Oct 1948, and Robert Coleman, in *New York Daily Mirror*, 7 Oct 1948 repr. in *New York Theatre Critics' Reviews, 1948*, pp. 205–6 and 208; Joseph Wood Krutch, in *Nation*, 167 (23 Oct 1948) 473–4; Harold Clurman, in *New Republic*, 119 (25 Oct 1948) 25–6; (15 Nov 1948) 27–8; *Time*, 52 (18 Oct 1948) 82–3; John Mason Brown in *Saturday Review*, 31 (30 Oct 1948) 31–3.

7. 'Cat on a Hot Tin Roof'

1. Peter Hoffman, 'The Last Days of Tennessee Williams', *New York*, 25 July 1983, p. 45.

2. The point is implicit in Ganz's penetrating discussion of Williams in *Realms of the Self* (New York: New York University Press, 1980). See pp. 114–15.

3. *Where I Live* (New York: New Directions, 1978) p. 21.

4. For details of the physical production, see Robert Downing, 'From the *Cat*–Bird Seat', *Theatre Annual*, 14 (1956) 46–50.

5. The cited reviews of *Cat on a Hot Tin Roof* are: Eric Bentley, in *New Republic*, 132 (11 Apr 1955), repr. in *What is Theatre? Incorporating The Dramatic Event and Other Reviews 1944–1967* (New York: Atheneum, 1968) pp. 224–31; Henry Hewes, in *Saturday Review*, 38 (9 Apr 1955) 32–3; Richard Watts, Jr, in *New York Post*, 25 Mar 1955, and Walter Kerr,

New York Herald-Tribune, 25 Mar 1955, repr. in *New York Theatre Critics' Reviews, 1955*, pp. 342–4; Walter Kerr, in *New York Times*, 6 Oct 1974, repr. in *New York Times Theatre Reviews, 1973–4*, pp. 280–1.

6. Downing, in *Theatre Annual*, 14, p. 48.

8. Wanderer Plays

1. The ballad is not reprinted in the play. See *In the Winter of Cities* (New York: New Directions, 1964) p. 101.

2. Ibid., p. 112.

9. Reversals of the Pattern

1. See Williams's poem 'Little Horse' in *In the Winter of Cities*, p. 120.

2. See 'Orpheus Descending', ibid., pp. 27–8.

10. Late Plays

1. The play derives from the short story 'Man Bring this up Road' (1959). See *Knightly Quest* (New York: New Directions, 1966) pp. 125–43.

2. All have the same name. For the one-act play, see *Esquire*, LXVI (Feb 1967) 98–100, 132–4. For the short story, see *Knightly Quest*, pp. 147–65.

3. *Vieux Carré* (New York: New Directions, 1979).

4. *A Lovely Sunday for Creve Coeur* (New York: New Directions, 1980).

5. *Clothes for a Summer Hotel* (New York: New Directions, 1983).

6. *Stopped Rocking and Other Screenplays* (New York: New Directions, 1984).

7. In *Christopher Street*, v, no. 10 (Nov 1981) 32–40.

Select Bibliography

(i) Works by Williams

Williams's publisher is New Directions in the United States and Secker and Warburg in the United Kingdom. Acting-editions are published by the Dramatists Play Service in New York. Paperbacks of some of the plays are also published, singly or in small collections, by the New American Library (Signet) and by Penguin Books Ltd.

DRAMA

The fullest edition, consulted for this study, is *The Theatre of Tennessee Williams*, 7 vols (New York: New Directions, 1971–81; Toronto: McClelland and Stewart, 1971–6 [I–V], and George J. McLeod, 1981 [VI–VII]). The key supplementary items are as follows.

American Blues (New York: Dramatists Play Service, 1948).
At Liberty, in *American Scenes*, ed. W. Kozlenko (New York: John Day, 1941) pp. 175–82.
Baby Doll (New York: New Directions, 1956; London: Secker and Warburg, 1957).
Clothes for a Summer Hotel (New York: New Directions, 1983).
The Enemy: Time, Theatre, I, no. 3 (Mar 1959) 14–17.
Kingdom of Earth (one act), *Esquire*, LXVI (Feb 1967) 98–100, 132–4.
Lord Byron's Love Letter (libretto), music by R. de Banfield (New York: Ricordi, 1955).

175

A Lovely Sunday for Creve Coeur (New York: New Directions, 1980).
Stopped Rocking and Other Screenplays (New York: New Directions, 1984).
A Streetcar Named Desire (screenplay), adaptation by O. Saul, in *Film Scripts. One*, ed. G. P. Garrett *et al.* (New York: Appleton-Century-Crofts, 1971) pp. 330–484.
The Travelling Companion, Christopher Street, v, no. 10 (Nov 1981) 32–40.
Vieux Carré (New York: New Directions, 1979).
You Touched Me!, written with D. Windham (New York: Samuel French, 1947).

POETRY AND PROSE

Androgyne, Mon Amour: Selected Poems (New York: New Directions, 1977).
Eight Mortal Ladies Possessed: A Book of Stories (New York: New Directions, 1974; London: Secker and Warburg, 1974).
Hard Candy: A Book of Stories (New York: New Directions, 1954).
In the Winter of Cities: Poems (New York: New Directions, 1964).
The Knightly Quest: A Novella and Four Short Stories (New York: New Directions, 1966).
Letters to Donald Windham 1940–65, ed. with comments by D. Windham (New York: Holt, Rinehart and Winston, 1977).
'The Man in the Overstuffed Chair', *Antaeus*, 45–6 (Spring–Summer 1982) 281–92.
Memoirs (New York: Doubleday, 1975; London: W. H. Allen, 1976).
Moise and the World of Reason (New York: Simon and Schuster, 1975; London: W. H. Allen, 1976).
One Arm and Other Stories (New York: New Directions, 1954).
The Roman Spring of Mrs Stone (New York: New Directions, 1950; London: John Lehman, 1950).
Where I Live: Selected Essays, ed. C. R. Day and B. Woods (New York: New Directions, 1978).

(ii) Works about Williams

BIBLIOGRAPHICAL

The most complete and up-to-date bibliography of works by and about Williams is Drewey Wayne Gunn, *Tennessee Williams: A Bibliography* (Metuchen, NJ: Scarecrow, 1980). But since Gunn is unfortunately full of errors the reader will find the following lists useful:

Select Bibliography

Carpenter, Charles A., 'Studies of Tennessee Williams's Drama: A Selective International Bibliography', *Tennessee Williams Newsletter*, II, no. 2 (Spring 1980) 11–23. Since 1974 Carpenter has included material on Williams in 'Modern Drama Studies: An Annual Bibliography', usually a feature of the June issue of *Modern Drama*.

McCann, John S., *The Critical Reputation of Tennessee Williams: A Reference Guide* (Boston, Mass.: G. K. Hall, 1983).

CRITICAL AND BIOGRAPHICAL: BOOKS

Donahue, Francis, *The Dramatic World of Tennessee Williams* (New York: Ungar, 1964).

Falk, Signi, *Tennessee Williams*, 2nd edn (Boston, Mass.: Twayne, 1978).

Hirsch, Foster, *A Portrait of the Artist: The Plays of Tennessee Williams* (Port Washington, NY: Kennikat, 1979).

Jackson, Esther M., *The Broken World of Tennessee Williams* (Madison, Milwaukee and London: University of Wisconsin Press, 1965).

Leavitt, Richard F., *The World of Tennessee Williams* (New York: Putnam, 1978; London: W. H. Allen, 1978).

Londré, Felicia H., *Tennessee Williams* (New York: Ungar, 1979).

Nelson, Benjamin, *Tennessee Williams: The Man and His Work* (New York: Obolensky, 1961), *Tennessee Williams: His Life and Work* (London: Peter Owens, 1961).

Phillips, Gene D., *The Films of Tennessee Williams* (Philadelphia: Art Alliance Press, 1980).

Spoto, Donald, *The Kindness of Strangers: The Life of Tennessee Williams* (Boston and Toronto: Little, Brown, 1985).

Tennessee Williams: A Collection of Critical Essays, ed. Stephen S. Stanton (Englewood Cliffs, NJ: Prentice-Hall, 1977).

Tennessee Williams: A Tribute, ed. Jac Tharpe (Jackson: University Press of Mississippi, 1977).

'The Glass Menagerie': A Collection of Critical Essays, ed. R. B. Parker (Englewood Cliffs, NJ: Prentice-Hall, 1983).

Tischler, Nancy M., *Tennessee Williams: Rebellious Puritan* (New York: Citadel, 1961).

Twentieth Century Interpretations of 'A Streetcar Named Desire', ed. Jordan Y. Miller (Englewood Cliffs, NJ: Prentice-Hall, 1971).

Weales, Gerald, *Tennessee Williams* (Minneapolis: University of Minnesota Press, 1965).

Williams, Dakin, and Mead, S., *Tennessee Williams: An Intimate Biography* (New York: Arbor House, 1983).

Williams, Edwina, as told to L. Freeman, *Remember me to Tom* (New York: Putnam, 1963; London: Cassell, 1964).

Tennessee Williams

CRITICAL AND BIOGRAPHICAL: ARTICLES AND PORTIONS OF BOOKS

Bentley, Eric, *In Search of Theatre* (New York: Atheneum, 1975) pp. 33–4, 87–9.

——, *What is Theatre? Incorporating the Dramatic Event and Other Reviews, 1944–67* (New York: Atheneum, 1968) pp. 71–2, 74–8, 224–31, 412–13 *et passim*.

Brandt, George, 'Cinematic Structure in the Work of Tennessee Williams' in *American Theatre* ed. J. R. Brown and B. Harris (London: Edward Arnold, 1967) pp. 163–87.

Cohn, Ruby, *Dialogue in American Drama* (Bloomington: Indiana University Press, 1971) pp. 97–129.

——, 'Late Tennessee Williams', *Modern Drama*, xxvii 3 (September 1984) 336–44.

Ganz, Arthur, *Realms of the Self: Variations on a Theme in Modern Drama* (New York and London: New York University Press, 1980) pp. 107–22.

Hoffman, Peter, as told to A. Shreve and F. Waitzkin, 'The Last Days of Tennessee Williams', *New York Magazine*, 25 July 1983, pp. 41–9.

Kazan, Elia, 'Notebook for *A Streetcar Named Desire*', in *Directors on Directing*, ed. T. Cole and H. C. Chinoy, rev. edn (Indianapolis: Bobbs-Merrill, 1963; London: Peter Owen, 1970).

Popkin, Henry, 'The Plays of Tennessee Williams', *Tulane Drama Review*, iv (Spring 1960) 45–64.

Vidal, Gore, 'Selected Memories of the Glorious Bird and the Golden Age', *New York Review of Books*, 5 Feb 1976, pp. 13–18.

(iii) Additional Material

Most of Williams's unpublished manuscripts are at the Humanities Research Center of the University of Texas at Austin. A number of unpublished and unproduced scripts, including an unfinished verse play written in the early 1940s (*A Balcony in Ferrara*), are in the office of the author's agent at International Creative Management in New York. Williams's remaining papers were left to Harvard.

Index

Index

Index

Index

Index

Index

Index

Index